# THE COMEDYSPORTZ® GAMES MANUAL

A GUIDE TO SHORT-FORM IMPROV GAMES

Compiled, Written, and Edited by Matthew Russell

Games Created by The People Who Created Them

**CSz Portland Editing Team:**

Jaye Rambo

Patrick Short

Leann Ruth Johnson

Jamie Montgomery

Andrew Berkowitz

Version 5.01 May, 2023

ISBN: 978-1-312-62932-5

© 2023 CSz Worldwide

**CSz® and ComedySportz® are registered trademarks of CSz Worldwide.**

All rights reserved.

No part of this book may be reproduced in any form or by any electronic or mechanical means, including information storage and retrieval systems, without written permission from CSz Worldwide, except for the use of brief quotations in a book review.

*ComedySportz* and the ComedySportz match format are registered trademarks of CSz Worldwide. Used with permission. Only ComedySportz licensees may perform ComedySportz—either by name or by format. Please visit cszworldwide.com for more information.

A limited right of performance of the material contained herein accompanies the purchase of this book. This right is limited to performances under an active ComedySportz license as authorized by CSz Worldwide.

Thank you for wearing nice shoes.

Matthew Russell thanks the following people and groups:

- Jaye Rambo, you're amazing. Thank you for helping me compile the games list, which I expanded into this guide, and so much else for this book.

- CSz Worldwide and those who invented the games found within this book. You are amazing.

## From the Editors

Matt Russell loved ComedySportz. He was a player, ref, teacher, announcer, team founder and mentor in Sacramento and—committing to the bit—both Portland, Oregon and Portland, Maine. On stage, he was the ultimate package, a showstopping performer who could use his encyclopedic knowledge to bust out a rap about 18th century economic policy before pivoting into a perfect impression of an anime dragon. Off stage, he was dedicated to his teammates, the kind of friend who would send random funny texts at all hours just to cheer you up.

Matt never met a ComedySportz game he didn't love. In fact, you'd often find him scheming before the match on a new game idea that had just popped into his head on the drive over, trying to talk his teammates into giving it a go right there on the spot. Some of these game ideas were amazing; many were absurd. That was Matt Russell in a nutshell.

Tragically, Matt passed away in 2022, before this book could be published. He had written the manual as a gift to the community, a labor of love from someone who loved CSz and all the games. After some light editing, we're now thrilled to get it into your hands. Please honor Matt's memory by playing these games with joy and commitment.

And remember to do a few bits.

Visit ComedySportz and CSz Worldwide:

comedysportz.com

cszworldwide.com

# TABLE OF CONTENTS

**WRITE YOUR OWN FOREWARD** ............................................................................................... 11
**HOW TO USE THE GUIDE** ........................................................................................................ 12
**TEAM GAMES** ............................................................................................................................ 15
    INTERRUPT GAMES ............................................................................................................. 17
        *ALEXA* ................................................................................................................................ 18
        *ARE YOU THINKING WHAT I'M THINKING?* ................................................................ 19
        *BACK TO WHENEVER* ..................................................................................................... 20
        *BIG LITTLE* ....................................................................................................................... 21
        *CHANGING EMOTIONS* ................................................................................................. 22
        *CONJUNCTION JUNCTION* ........................................................................................... 23
        *D&D IN THE LIFE* ........................................................................................................... 24
        *DEEPER* ............................................................................................................................ 25
        *FORWARD REVERSE* ....................................................................................................... 26
        *FOURSQUARE* ................................................................................................................. 27
        *FREEZE TAG* .................................................................................................................... 28
        *GROWING SHRINKING MACHINE* ............................................................................... 29
        *I DREAM OF JEANNIE* .................................................................................................... 30
        *I GOTTA TAKE THIS* ....................................................................................................... 31
        *IDENTITY CRISIS* ............................................................................................................. 32
        *INNER MONOLOGUE* .................................................................................................... 33
        *INTERRUPTING ZEBRA* ................................................................................................. 34
        *NEW CHOICE* .................................................................................................................. 35
        *NITTY BRITTY* .................................................................................................................. 36
        *OLD TIME COMIC* .......................................................................................................... 37
        *OSCAR WINNING MOMENT* ........................................................................................ 38
        *PARALLEL UNIVERSE* ..................................................................................................... 39
        *SCANTRON* ...................................................................................................................... 40
        *SOAP OPERA* ................................................................................................................... 41
        *SPIN-OFF* ......................................................................................................................... 42
        *START OVER* ..................................................................................................................... 43
        *STUNT DOUBLE* .............................................................................................................. 44
        *SWITCH* ............................................................................................................................ 45
        *SYNONYM ROLLS* .......................................................................................................... 46
        *TAG TEAM MONOLOGUE* ............................................................................................ 47
    REPLAY GAMES ..................................................................................................................... 49
        *BASIC REPLAY* ................................................................................................................. 50
        *BIG FISH* ........................................................................................................................... 51
        *COUNTDOWN* ................................................................................................................ 52
        *ELIMINATOR REPLAY* .................................................................................................... 53
        *GROUNDHOG'S REPLAY* ............................................................................................... 54
        *GROUNDHOG'S REPLAY* ............................................................................................... 55
        *MULTIPLICITY* ................................................................................................................. 56
        *MULTIVERSE* .................................................................................................................... 57

  *NAIVE REPLAY* ............................................................................................ *58*
  *REPLAY AT BERNIE'S* ............................................................................ *59*
  *SKEWED* .................................................................................................. *60*
  *TEMPORAL REPLAY* ............................................................................... *61*

## JUSTIFICATION GAMES ............................................................................... 63
  *ACROMANIA* ........................................................................................... *64*
  *DIME STORE NOVEL* ............................................................................. *65*
  *INTERPRETER* ........................................................................................ *66*
  *INSTANT SOAP OPERA* ........................................................................ *67*
  *LIMIT LINE* .............................................................................................. *68*
  *MEMENTO* ............................................................................................... *69*
  *OFFSTAGE DIRECTIONS* ...................................................................... *70*
  *OXYGEN DEPRIVATION (18+)* ............................................................ *71*
  *PAVLOVIAN RESPONSE* ....................................................................... *72*
  *PICK A PLAY* ........................................................................................... *73*
  *PICK-UP LINES* ....................................................................................... *74*
  *REVOLVING DOORS* ............................................................................. *75*
  *SIT STAND KNEEL LIE* .......................................................................... *76*
  *STAND BY SCENE* .................................................................................. *77*
  *SUBTEXT* ................................................................................................. *78*
  *UNCLE GIBBERISH* ............................................................................... *79*

## VOLUNTEER PLAYER GAMES .................................................................... 81
  *ARMS EXPERT (18 +)* ............................................................................ *82*
  *AUDIENCE SOUND EFFECTS* .............................................................. *83*
  *BEDTIME STORY* .................................................................................... *84*
  *COFFEE BREAK* ...................................................................................... *85*
  *COLUMNS* ................................................................................................ *86*
  *DAY IN THE LIFE* .................................................................................... *87*
  *DINNER AT JOE'S* .................................................................................. *88*
  *DOUBLE SPEAK* ..................................................................................... *89*
  *FOREIGN MOVIE* ................................................................................... *90*
  *LAUGHTERHOUSE 5* .............................................................................. *91*
  *MOVING BODIES* ................................................................................... *92*
  *NEWSCASTER* ........................................................................................ *93*
  *SLIDE SHOW* .......................................................................................... *94*
  *SLO-MO* ................................................................................................... *95*
  *TALK RADIO* ........................................................................................... *96*
  *THE EVENT* ............................................................................................. *97*
  *WHAT IF?* ................................................................................................ *98*
  *WORD FROM OUR SPONSOR* ............................................................ *99*

## MUSICAL GAMES ........................................................................................ 101
  *AUDIENCE & HAMMERSTEIN* ........................................................... *102*
  *BLANK! THE MUSICAL* ....................................................................... *103*
  *GIBBERISH OPERA* ............................................................................. *104*
  *IPSO FACTO OPERA* ........................................................................... *105*
  *LOUNGE LIZARDS* ............................................................................... *106*
  *MADRIGAL* ............................................................................................ *107*
  *MUSICAL GENRE* ................................................................................. *108*
  *PIANO TORTURE* ................................................................................. *109*
  *SCHOOLHOUSE MOCK* ....................................................................... *110*

- SHAM-ILTON ... 111
- SING IT ... 112
- THAT SOUNDS LIKE A SONG ... 113
- THREE-HEADED BROADWAY STAR ... 114
- TIN PAN ALLEY ... 115

CATCH-ALL GAMES ... 117
- AB SCENE ... 118
- ACRONYM PANEL ... 119
- ADVICE PANEL ... 120
- ALPHABET GENRE ... 121
- BUZZFEED ... 122
- CRITIC ... 123
- DR. KNOW-IT-ALL ... 124
- DUBBING ... 125
- EMOTIONAL ROLLERCOASTER ... 126
- EMOTIONAL SYMPHONY ... 127
- FINISHING SCHOOL ... 128
- FLASH PHRASE ... 129
- GAME-O-MATIC ... 130
- GENRE PIECE ... 131
- IF BLANKS RULED THE WORLD ... 132
- MARSHMALLOW (18+) ... 133
- MOUSETRAP (18+) ... 134
- MUNDANE ZOMBIE ATTACK ... 135
- MY MOVIE ... 136
- NO SEE, NO HEAR, NO SPEAK ... 137
- REMAKE ... 138
- SEARS FAMILY PORTRAIT ... 139
- SPELLING BEE ... 140
- SPORK RIVER ... 141
- STUDIO AUDIENCE ... 142
- SUPERHERO EULOGY ... 143
- TAKE MY PANTS ... 144
- TOOTS MCGOOTS ... 145

# GUESSING GAMES ... 147
- ANIMATRONIC JAMBOREE ... 148
- BLITZ ... 149
- CHAIN MURDER ... 150
- CRYSTAL BALL ... 151
- DATING GAME ... 152
- FIVE THINGS ... 153
- HOSTAGE NEGOTIATOR ... 155
- HOT BELL ... 156
- INTERROGATION ... 157
- LIE DETECTOR ... 158
- MYSTERY WHERE ... 159
- NIGHT AT THE BALLET ... 160
- STICKER-DOODLES ... 161
- THE QUEST ... 162

## HEAD-TO-HEAD GAMES ... 164
### SCENIC HEAD-TO-HEAD GAMES ... 166
- *15 SECONDS EARLIER* ... 167
- *55 WORDS* ... 168
- *BATTLESCENE GALACTICA* ... 169
- *CONTINUATION* ... 170
- *DANCE PARTY* ... 171
- *DICK VAN DYKE* ... 172
- *DON'T MAKE ME HECKLE* ... 173
- *ECHO* ... 174
- *FOREIGN TELEVISION* ... 175
- *GOOGLE TRANSLATE* ... 176
- *GRAND THEFT AUTO* ... 177
- *I CAN DO BETTER* ... 178
- *I GIVE UP* ... 179
- *LAUGH OUT* ... 180
- *MEANWHILE, ELSEWHERE* ... 181
- *MIRROR, MIRROR* ... 182
- *PEN PALS* ... 183
- *QUESTIONS ONLY* ... 184
- *SCOOP IT* ... 185
- *STORY* ... 186
- *SWITCH INTERVIEW* ... 187
- *THREE ROOMS* ... 188
- *TWO CHAIRS* ... 189
- *WORD AT A TIME EXPRESS* ... 190
- *WORLD WITHOUT A LETTER* ... 191
- *YAY BOO* ... 192

### CATCH-ALL HEAD-TO-HEAD GAMES ... 194
- *AUDITION* ... 195
- *CASANOVA (18+)* ... 196
- *RADIO* ... 197
- *SCATTERGORIES* ... 198
- *SWIPE RIGHT* ... 199
- *TOWN HALL / TOWN MEETING* ... 200
- *TRY THAT ON FOR SIZE* ... 201
- *TWO MINUTE EXPERT* ... 202
- *WHAT ARE YOU DOING?* ... 203

### MUSICAL HEAD-TO-HEAD GAMES ... 205
- *BEASTIE RAP / RUN DMC* ... 206
- *CELEBRITY JAM* ... 207
- *COMPILATION ALBUM* ... 208
- *DA DOO RON RON* ... 209
- *DANCE PARTY* ... 211
- *DUELING SOUNDTRACKS* ... 212
- *MUSICAL RUMBLE* ... 213
- *RHYME LINE* ... 214
- *SING FOR YOUR SUPPER* ... 215
- *WHAT YOU GOT?* ... 216

### GUESSING HEAD-TO-HEAD GAMES ... 218

| | |
|---|---|
| *GUESS THAT THING* | 219 |
| *I LOVE A PARADE* | 220 |
| *PLAYGROUND INSULTS* | 221 |

## LAST CHANCE GAMES ............................................................................................ 223

| | |
|---|---|
| *185* | 224 |
| *BACK IN MY DAY* | 225 |
| *B MOVIE* | 226 |
| *COMING SOON...* | 227 |
| *CRAIGSLIST* | 228 |
| *DEAR DIARY,* | 229 |
| *FANDAMONIUM* | 230 |
| *GAME OF GROANS* | 231 |
| *GARTH* | 232 |
| *HEY, WAITER* | 233 |
| *I KISSED A BLANK* | 234 |
| *IT'S NOT YOU, IT'S ME* | 235 |
| *JERSEY DINER* | 236 |
| *JIMMY THE PIGEON* | 237 |
| *LAST ACTION JOKE* | 238 |
| *LET ME TELL YOU SOMETHING, BROTHER* | 239 |
| *LETTERS FROM CAMP* | 240 |
| *OBJECT FREEZE* | 241 |
| *PHONE HOME* | 242 |
| *SMACKDOWN* | 243 |
| *TSA* | 244 |
| *WHATCHA GET?* | 245 |
| *WHEN I GROW UP* | 246 |
| *WORLD'S WORST* | 247 |

## STREAMING GAMES ............................................................................................... 249

| | |
|---|---|
| *ANTIQUES ROADSHOW* | 250 |
| *DIRECTOR'S COMMENTARY* | 251 |
| *DUB CLUB* | 252 |
| *GRAMMA-PHONE* | 253 |
| *MISGUIDED MEDITATION* | 254 |
| *NEAR, FAR, WHEREVER YOU ARE* | 255 |
| *PASS THE MIC* | 256 |
| *PIF (PUBLIC INFORMATION FILM)* | 257 |
| *SORKIN* | 258 |
| *SPECIAL DELIVERY* | 259 |
| *TELEPROMPTER MUSICAL* | 260 |

## GAME LISTS .............................................................................................................. 262

| | |
|---|---|
| TEAM GAMES LIST | 263 |
|    INTERRUPT GAMES | 263 |
|    REPLAY GAMES | 265 |
|    JUSTIFICATION GAMES | 265 |
|    VOLUNTEER PLAYER GAMES | 266 |
|    MUSICAL GAMES | 267 |
|    CATCH-ALL | 268 |

*GUESSING GAMES* ............................................................................................................ *270*
HEAD-TO-HEAD GAMES LIST ................................................................................. 271
  *SCENIC HEAD-TO-HEAD GAMES* ................................................................................ *271*
  *CATCH-ALL HEAD-TO-HEAD GAMES* ......................................................................... *272*
  *MUSICAL HEAD-TO-HEAD GAMES* ............................................................................ *273*
  *GUESSING HEAD-TO-HEAD GAMES* .......................................................................... *273*
  *LAST CHANCE GAMES* ............................................................................................... *274*
  *STREAMING GAMES* .................................................................................................. *275*

# WRITE YOUR OWN FOREWARD

# HOW TO USE THE GUIDE

Games-based improv, also known as *short-form improv*, is a style of improvisational comedy that utilizes games while performing completely unscripted scenes. This style of improvisational comedy has been popularized by such popular live shows as ComedySportz®, Theatresports™, and the Canadian Improv Games. It is also seen on television programs including *Whose Line Is It Anyway* and *Wild 'n Out*. This guide is a playbook of many of the games played in matches at ComedySportz® matches all over the world, and is written with that style in mind.

The games are separated into two main sections: Team Games and Head-to-Head Games. Each of these sections is then organized into categories.

The first of these sections is Team Games. These are games that are generally played in the Team Choice/Team Challenge Round by a team of three-four players. This section has been organized into seven categories: Interrupts, Replays, Justification, Musical, Volunteer Player, Guessing, and Catch All

The second is Head-To-Head Games. These are games that are played in the other rounds of the match when both teams would play together. This section has been organized into five main categories: Scenic Head-To-Heads, Musical Head-To-Heads, Catch-All Head-to-Heads, Guessing Head-to-Heads, and Last Chance.

Here is an example game description:

# NAME OF GAME

*"Sample Referee Intro"*

The basic way as to how the game is played. This is given with minimal tips/tricks as to allow players to find those, as the discovery of them leads to making the game your own.
**Alternate Names:** If there are any they will go here.

**Variations on this Game**

- If there is an alternate version of this game which is different enough from the basic version, the explanation it will be here.

- If there are any variations played by cities, it will also be found here.

- If it can be easily translated to a Head-To-Head Game it will be here with any rule changes to the variation, if any.

- If it can be played with a volunteer player, it will be here with any variation rule changes, if any.

- (If the variant is named differently it will be in parenthesis in quotes)


Special Note: If the game has a (18+) next to the name, it should only be played by those of that age.

If a game you are looking for doesn't have its own entry, chances are it is explained as a variation of a game that does. Try looking for a similar game, or use our index in the back that includes where to find all the games in this book. If it still isn't found there, use the included blank pages found at the end of each section and at the end of the book, to add it in. (Do not attempt this if you are using a digital copy. Writing on your screen generally won't work.)

Speaking of defacing a book, also feel free to write in the book next to the games or anywhere you wish. Fill in any tips, tricks, bits, or best practices you have found that work best for you or your team. (Again, do not attempt this if you are using a digital copy. Seriously, electronics are expensive.)

While this book is geared towards the ComedySportz® style of gameplay, if you are not affiliated with ComedySportz® you can still use this book as a helpful resource for games. Simply ignore the stuff about match structure, and replace the words "Referee" with "Host," "Volunteer Player" with "Audience Volunteer," and "Field" with "Stage." Under no circumstance should you market your show as a ComedySportz® match unless you have the appropriate license to do so. If you wish to become licensed to use the ComedySportz® name and trade dress, please contact CSz Worldwide for more information.

# TEAM GAMES

In any given home match, the teams will play at least four Team Games. Having a mix of the categories here will lead to a more balanced match, or at least be sure to look at the objective of the games, their stage picture, and how they are played when choosing the games.

- Interrupt - These are games where the primary objective is having the flow of the scene/game be interrupted by the referee or another player.

- Replay - These are games where the primary objective is replaying a neutral scene in different ways.

- Justification - These are games where the primary objective is to justify any internal or external forces on the scene.

- Volunteer Player - These are games where the primary objective is to utilize a volunteer player. While these games can be easily put in other categories as well, they fall into this category as they share the volunteer player aspect.

- Musical - These are games where the primary objective is to utilize music. While these games can be easily put in other categories as well, as they all share the music aspect.

- Catch All - These are games where the primary objective is just in a world of its own, or they are too difficult to put into just one of the other categories. For simplicity's sake, they are gathered here.

- Guessing - These are games where the primary objective is to showcase guessing and clue giving.

# INTERRUPT GAMES

Interrupt games are games that utilize the referee or another player to change the flow of the game. Generally, the interrupt games listed here are played by a single team during the Team Choice/Team Challenge round.

# ALEXA

*"The players will do a scene, and whenever they wish they can ask Alexa a question. After Alexa answers, they will begin a new scene based on the answer."*

The referee gets a suggestion for the game, and the players start a neutral scene. At some point in the scene, one player will stop and ask "Alexa" a question about something in the scene, based on the answer, a new scene will begin. This repeats until time is called. "Alexa" can either be the other team, the announcer, or the referee.

**Alternate Names:** *Hey Siri*

**Variations on this Game**

• May be played in a Head-To-Head round, with the teams switching scene initiations between Alexa's answers.

# ARE YOU THINKING WHAT I'M THINKING?

*"Every so often the players will share a thought, and must justify it into the world."*

The referee gets a suggestion for the game, and the players start a neutral scene. Every so often a player says, "Are you thinking what I'm thinking?" When this is said, all players in the scene look at each other and begin to speak in unison, sharing their thought. They must then justify this new information into the scene.

**Variations on this Game**

- May be played with the referee interrupting the players to have them say "Are you thinking what I'm thinking?", and give them a one syllable sound to start with.

# BACK TO WHENEVER

*"The players will do a scene, and whenever I want more backstory I can blow my whistle and take the scene back to whenever."*

The referee gets a suggestion for the game and the players begin a neutral scene. Whenever the referee wishes, after a player gives an offer of an event in the past, they may interrupt the scene and declare "Back to ___!" The players will then take the scene back in time to give more backstory to what was said. This repeats as the referee takes us further back in time or back to the present.

**Alternate Names:** *Flashback*

# BIG LITTLE

*"The team will do a scene, and throughout it I can blow my whistle and demand they make the scene 'Little' or 'Big'"*

A chair or stool is placed on the field. The referee gets a suggestion for the game, and the players begin with a neutral scene. Whenever the referee wishes, they may interrupt the scene to change its size. When "Little," the players enact the scene using their fingers on the chair, index and middle fingers are to be used as their character's legs. When "Big," the players return to their normal size. The size change allows for players to do extraordinary things while "Little," and these actions shape the new reality.

# CHANGING EMOTIONS

*"The team will do a scene, and throughout it I can blow my whistle and change the emotional state of one or all of the players."*

The referee gets a list of multiple emotions. They then get a suggestion for the game, and the players begin with a neutral scene. Whenever the referee wishes, they may interrupt the game to layer on one of the emotions. Whenever a new one is given by the referee, the previous emotion is dropped by the players.

**Variations on this Game**

- May be played with the referee getting the suggestions for the changes throughout the scene as opposed to all at once.

- May be played with the referee assigning the change to only one specific player.

- May be played with accents instead of emotions. (Called "*Accent Roller Coaster*" or "*Changing Voices*")

- May be played time periods instead of emotions. (Called "*Fabric of Time*")

- May be played with the referee getting a list of emotions, genres, time periods, voices, etc. (Called "*Changing Styles,*" "*Changing Emotions and Stuff,*" or "*Changing Genres*")

- May be played with the previous styles, emotions, and such are layered upon each other. (Called "*Pileup*")

# CONJUNCTION JUNCTION

*"The team will do a scene, and throughout it I can blow my whistle and ask players to add more to their previous offer with an additional conjunction."*

The referee gets a suggestion for the game, and the players begin with a neutral scene. Whenever the referee wishes, they may interrupt the scene and call on a specific player, giving them a conjunction, such as "and," "or," "because," etc. That player must add to their last offer by expanding upon it utilizing the conjunction given.

# D&D IN THE LIFE

*"They team will do a scene and every so often they players will ask to see how well they do. I will roll a 20-sided die and the higher the number the better they do."*

The referee gets a suggestion for a scene, and they begin neutrally. When the players feel like it, they will ask for the referee to "check" how well they do for specific things. These can be reactions, actions, emotional responses, etc. The referee will roll a 20-sided die, and tell the number to the players; on a 1 it is the worse it can possibly go, on a 20 it is the best. Referee may fudge the numbers as they see needed.

# DEEPER

*"The team will do a scene, and throughout it I can blow my whistle and ask players to add deeper context to their previous offer."*

The referee gets a suggestion for the game, and the players begin with a neutral scene. Whenever the referee wishes, they may interrupt the scene and call on a specific player. That player must add to their last offer, action, or line provide deeper meaning or context by expanding upon it.

**Variations on this Game**

• May be played with the referee calling for the scene to get awkwarder. (Called *Awkwarder*)

# FORWARD REVERSE

*"The team will do a scene, and throughout it I can blow my whistle and change if the scene is going forward in time, or in reverse."*

The referee gets a suggestion for the game, and the players begin with a neutral scene. Whenever the referee wishes, they may interrupt the game and call out "Reverse!" When this happens, players must repeat their actions and lines (not words, but lines) in reverse order until the referee calls out "Forward!" and the players continue their scene forward.

**Variations on this Game**

- May be played with more commands, similar to those found on a DVD remote. (Called *DVD* or *Remote Control*)

- May be played with the players going Reverse in Shakespearean and common English when going Forward. (Called *Forward In Verse*)

- May be played going fully in reverse for 60-90 seconds, then forward through the whole thing once. (Called *Scene In Reverse*)

# FOURSQUARE

*"In groups of two, the players will do a series of different scenes, when I choose I can blow my whistle and rotate between."*

A team of four forms a square on the field with two in front, and two behind them. The referee will rotate between the pairs for each to get a suggestion. The two in front do a scene based of their suggestion, until the referee interrupts them to rotate left or right to change the scene. When two players are in the front again some amount of time will have passed in between now and when we last saw them.

**Alternate Names:** *Four Corners; Four Quadrants; Pan Left*

**Variations on this Game**

- May be played with three players, and include a volunteer player.

- May be played with the players behind dubbing for those in front. (Called *Foursquare Dubbing*)

- May be played with five players, or four with a volunteer player, with the fifth point providing sound effects. (Called *Foursquare Sound Effects*)

- May be played with a fifth player, or volunteer player, who is in every scene regardless of rotation. (Called *Pretty, Pretty Princess* or *Center Of Attention*)

- May be played with a musical variation, with each pair singing duets. (Called *Four Crooners* or *Duets*)

# FREEZE TAG

*"Two players will start a scene, and whenever another player chooses they may say 'Freeze.' The players will then freeze and the caller will tap out, take their exact position and start a new scene."*

The referee gets a suggestion for the game, and two players start a scene. Whenever another player wishes throughout the scene, they will yell "Freeze!" The on-field players must immediately freeze in position. The player that yelled freeze replaces one or more of the frozen players. A new scene begins, starting from that exact position.

**Alternate Names:** Freeze

**Variations on this Game**

- May be played with a volunteer player.

- May be played head-to-head.

- May be played with the players having their backs turned towards the field, essentially playing without looking. (Called *No-Peek Freeze Tag*)

- May be played using lines of dialogue as opposed to motions, the new scenes begin in any position but start with the last line of dialogue from the previous scene. (Called *Copycat*)

# GROWING SHRINKING MACHINE

*"One player will do a scene by themselves, and at any point I may blow my whistle to add or subtract players, and changing the scene."*

The referee will get a suggestion, and one player will begin a scene alone. Whenever the referee wishes, they may interrupt the game and call out either "Grow!" or "Shrink!". During growing another player will join, establishing a new scene based on the suggestion, this is the establish reality whenever there are that many players on the field for the rest of the game. When shrinking, one player will exit the field, and the scene reverts back to the scene created with that number of players. It grows until all players are on the field, then shrinks back down to one.

**Alternate Names:** Growing Shrinking **Variations on this Game**

- May be played going the opposite direction, starting with the whole team, shrinking to one, and growing back to the whole team. (Called *Shrinking Growing*)

- The referee may freeze the players and determine who leaves or enters, played almost like a structured freeze tag, including justification for position.

- May be played with the players entering and exiting scenes of their own accord, rather than having the referee involved.

- May be played head-to-head, alternating the addition of a player from each team each time. (Called *Mega Growing Shrinking Machine*)

# I DREAM OF JEANNIE

*"The players will begin a scene, and whenever the other team chooses, they may sing the I Dream of Jeannie theme, and make a wish. I can choose to grant or deny it."*

The referee gets a suggestion, and the players begin a neutral scene. Whenever the other team chooses, they will sing the I Dream of Jeannie song, and the referee will stand and say "Yes?" then the wish is made. The referee may grant, or choose not to grant any wish. The wishes affect the reality of the scene, and stay in place until wished away.

**Variations on this Game**

- May be played where all of the wishes have horrible consequences for the players. (Called *Jeannie's Nightmare*.)

- May be played without the Jeannie aspect, and the referee interrupting the scene, calling on anyone to make a rule, and the players continuing with the new rule. (Called *Calvin Ball*)

# I GOTTA TAKE THIS

*"The players will begin a scene, and whenever the other team chooses, they may phone one of the players in the scene to change it."*

The referee gets a suggestion, and the players begin a neutral scene. Whenever the other team chooses, they will make the sound of a ringtone and one of the players on the field will answer their phone. The player who made the "call" will provide them with information which can change the scene, be it tactics, a secret, or whatever they wish, and this becomes reality in the scene. Each player on the field, will receive one phone call, and each player of the other team will only make one.

# IDENTITY CRISIS

*"The team will do a scene, and throughout it I can blow my whistle and change who is playing which character."*

The referee gets a suggestion for the game, and a genre. The players begin with a neutral scene, each playing strong, and distinct characters. Whenever the referee wishes, they may blow their whistle and call "Switch," forcing all the players to switch who is playing which role. This process repeats and continues until the game has ended.

**Alternate Names:** *Heavy Rotation*

**Variations on this Game**

May be played with the referee getting suggestions for each character as well.

May be played with each player wearing a hat to designate who is playing what character.

• May be played with the hats, and the endowments attached to said hat switching, but the characters not switching player. (Called *Hats*)

# INNER MONOLOGUE

*"The players will begin a scene, and throughout it I can blow my whistle and call for a specific player to share their character's inner-monologue."*

The referee gets a suggestion for the game, and the players begin with a neutral scene. Whenever the referee wishes, they may interrupt the game and call out a player. That player will step-forward and share their character's inner-monologue. During their monologue, the other players stand still, and do not acknowledge this break has happened, and while the players have heard the monologue, their characters have not. Either the referee or player may end the monologue and continue the scene with the new information.

**Alternate Names:** *Penny For Your Thoughts*

**Variations on this Game**

- May be played head-to-head with the players partnered with a player on the other team, who provide each other's inner-monologue when called upon.

- May be played where the player must sing their thoughts. (Called *Inner Songologue*)

# INTERRUPTING ZEBRA

*"The players will begin a scene, and throughout it I can blow my whistle and make any changes I wish with a variety of commands."*

The referee gets a suggestion for the game, and the players begin with a neutral scene. Whenever the referee wishes, they may interrupt the game and call any command from any Interrupt Games. This includes "Forward," "Reverse," "New Choice," etc. The players on the field will react appropriately.

# NEW CHOICE

*"The players will begin a scene, and throughout it I can blow my whistle and call 'New Choice!' and the player will have to make a new choice."*

The referee gets a suggestion for the game, and the players begin with a neutral scene. Whenever the referee wishes, they may interrupt the game and say, "New Choice!" The player who just spoke/acted has to replace the last action/line with something completely different. The referee keeps going until they or the fans hear something they like, and this becomes the new reality of the scene.

**Variations on this Game**

- May be played with the new choices having to rhyme with the last line of dialogue as well. (Called *New Rhyme*)

- May be played with the players from the other team calling for the new choice by spraying the players with water bottles. (Called *Bad Kitty*)

# NITTY BRITTY

*"The players will begin a scene, and throughout it I can blow my whistle and call for them to become more or less British."*

The referee gets a suggestion for the game, and the players begin with a neutral scene. Whenever the referee wishes, they may interrupt the game and instruct the player to become more or less British. If a player is British, they will become more or less American.

# OLD TIME COMIC

*"The players will begin a scene, and throughout it I can blow my whistle and call out a word said by a player. From there it is a surprise."*

The referee gets a suggestion for the game, and the players begin with a neutral scene. Whenever the referee wishes, they may interrupt the game and call out a player and a word that was just used. That player will drop everything, jump out and declare in a Jimmy Durante-esque vaudevillian manner "Hey, Morty, did you hear the one about the (word called by referee)?" At this point, all players regardless of team will jump onto the field, and taking the same pose and voice clap their hands and respond "No, Morty, we didn't hear the one about the (word called by referee)" The original player will deliver a pun based on that word, and all players jazz hands and say "Ha-cha-cha" and leave the field. Play then continues as if nothing happened.

**Alternate Names:** *Hey Morty; Vaudeville; Old School Stand-Up*

# OSCAR WINNING MOMENT

*"The players will begin a scene, and throughout it I can blow my whistle and call out a player, who will then show us the Oscar winning moment from that scene."*

The referee gets a suggestion for the game, and the players begin with a neutral scene. Whenever the referee wishes, they may interrupt the game and call out a player who will then take a turn for the dramatic, delivering the moment that would be shown as to why they were nominated for an Oscar. Either the referee or the player may end the moment. This moment is part of the reality.

**Variations on this Game**

- May be played with commands such as Best Action Scene or Best Kiss. (Called *MTV Movie Awards* or *Teen Choice Awards*)

- May be played with the moments being sung in a Broadway fashion. (Called *Tony Winning Moment*)

# PARALLEL UNIVERSE

*"The players will begin a scene, and throughout it I can blow my whistle and call out a location, and the scene shifts to that location."*

The referee will get a list of three or four locations, chooses one as the starting point for the game, and the players begin a scene in that location. Whenever the referee wishes, they may interrupt the game and call out one of the other locations, and the players must justify their positions in that new location. The referee may also go to locations previously visited and the scenes that had been established there must continue with the new positions.

**Variations on this Game**

• May be played with the players dying in ridiculous ways, falling dead on the ground. When the locations shift, if a player is dead in that location they must quickly get back to where their body was, if they died in the scene previous but were alive in the other locations, they must justify why they were on the ground. The goal is to have all dead in all locations. (Called *Death Pendulum*)

# SCANTRON

*"The players will begin a scene, and throughout it I can blow my whistle and ask the players what happens next, then you all will choose between the answers."*

The referee gets a suggestion for the game, and the players begin with a neutral scene. Whenever the referee wishes, they may interrupt the game and ask the players what happens next, while hovering a hand over their heads. After all the players have had a chance to voice what they believe happens next, the audience will select their answer, and it happens almost instantly.

**Variations on this Game**

• May be interrupted by players who will put their hand their hand on a player and suggest a scene for the two of them to do together. The players with the hands on them selects where to go next. (Called *Choose Your Own Adventure*)

# SOAP OPERA

*"The players will perform a soap opera scene, and whenever they hear a musical sting, one character's inner thoughts will be exposed."*

The referee gets a suggestion for the game, places a stool center-field, and the players begin a scene in the style of a dramatic soap opera. Whenever the announcer wishes, they will play a dramatic sting, and one player will step to the stool looking towards the audience with a far-off gaze. The announcer then provides their innermost thoughts and secrets, which must be justified into the scene.

**Variations on this Game**

- May be played with the other team providing the inner thoughts of the players.

# SPIN-OFF

*"The team will perform a scene, and whenever I wish I can call for a character to have their own spin-off."*

The referee gets a suggestion for the game, and the players begin a neutral scene. Whenever the referee wishes, the will interrupt the scene and call for one of the characters to have a spin-off scene, and get a suggestion of a genre from the audience. The players now perform the new scene. This repeats until the end of the game.

**Variations on this Game**

- May be played head-to-head.

# START OVER

*"The team will perform a scene beginning with a specific action, and whenever I wish I can call for the game to start over."*

The referee gets a suggestion of a physical action for the game. The players will begin a scene where one player is doing the action, and the others making it make sense. Whenever the referee wishes, the will interrupt the scene and call for the players to "Start Over." When this happens, one player will begin doing the original activity, and a new scene starts. This repeats until the end of the game.

**Variations on this Game**

• May be played head-to-head with the teams switching each time the referee calls "Start Over."

# STUNT DOUBLE

*"The players will be doing a scene, and throughout it I can blow my whistle and call for stunt doubles for the dangerous stuff."*

The referee gets a suggestion for the game, and the players begin a with a neutral scene. Whenever the referee wishes, they may interrupt the game and call for a stunt double who will come in tap out a player and perform the next action in a highly over the top dangerous fashion. The stunt double may be a player from their team or the other team. The actions taken by the stunt double change the realty.

**Variations on this Game**

- May be interrupted by players rather than the referee.

- May be played with the referee calling for the "Evil Twin" instead, and a player from the other team taps out a player and does something evil. (Called *Evil Twin*)

# SWITCH

*"The team will do a scene, and throughout it I can blow my whistle and change their scene between normal and the genre."*

The referee gets a suggestion for the game, and a genre. The players begin with a neutral scene. Whenever the referee wishes, they may interrupt the game and call out "Switch!" and the players must immediately switch from their normal scene to the genre given, and vice- versa.

**Variations on this Game**

- May be played with a predetermined genre. (Called "___ Switch" depending on the predetermined genre.)

- May be played with switching between the style of speaking rather than the genre. (Called *Gibberish Switch*, *Shakespeare Switch*, *Seuss Switch*, *Rap Switch*, etc.)

- May be played with switching between two genres, such as Rapping and Shakespeare (Called *Slamlet*)

# SYNONYM ROLLS

*"The players will begin a scene, and throughout it I can blow my whistle and the players will begin to list synonyms for what they just said."*

The referee gets a suggestion for the game, and the players begin with a neutral scene. Whenever the referee wishes, they may interrupt the game and repeat a word, the player who said that word will begin to list synonyms for that word as quickly as possible. When the referee hears one they like, they will blow their whistle a second time (or say, "That's it!") and repeat the new word. From then forward anytime the original word should be said it is replaced with the synonym.

# TAG TEAM MONOLOGUE

*"The players will begin a monologue, however whenever they tap each other out they will switch who is telling the story."*

The referee gets a suggestion for the game, and the players line up behind one another. The player in the front begins to tell a story or monologue based on the suggestion, then at any point in time the player behind them will tap them on the shoulder and take over where they left off, as the same character. The tap-outs get faster as the game progresses.

**Variations on this Game**

- May be played head-to-head with one player acting out everything the other team says during their storytelling. The referee will switch between the teams telling the story and acting it out. (Called *Tag Team Tale*)

- Can be played as a musical, with players finishing each others lines and words in song. End with all singing together. (Called *Tag Team Musical*)

# GAMES NOT MENTIONED IN THIS SECTION

# REPLAY GAMES

Replay games are games that utilize a 60-90 second neutral setup scene as the starting point for rest of the game. Traditionally all of the games are replayed three times, hitting similar benchmarks each time. Generally, replay games are played by a single team during the Team Choice/Team Challenge round.

# BASIC REPLAY

(Start of the game) *"The players will play a short setup scene, and I will be back to explain the rest in a moment."*

(After getting the style suggestions) *"Now the players will replay the scene in the different styles."*

The referee gets a suggestion for the game, and the players begin with a neutral scene. After the scene is done, the referee will gather a list of styles for the players to replay the scene in. These can be genres of film, television, theatre, literature, or music. They can also get voices, accents, letters for alliteration, emotions, or animals for each of the players. The style of replay is really up to the referee.

After getting the three replay styles, the team playing the game chooses the order to do the replays in, mapping the new styles over the original scene.

**Alternate Names:** *Replay; Genre Replay*

**Variations on this Game**

- May be played head-to-head with the teams alternating when replaying the scenes. May do a new setup scene after each team has done a replay. (Called *Mega Replay*)

- May be played where the genres layer upon each other. (Called *Pileup Replay*)

# BIG FISH

(Start of the game) *"The players will play a short setup scene, and I will be back to explain the rest in a moment."*

(After getting the style suggestions) *"Now the players will replay the scene in a more exaggerated fashion."*

The referee gets a suggestion for the game, and the players begin with a neutral scene. After the scene is done, the referee will challenge them to make the scene more exaggerated. They replay the scene three times, making it more exaggerated each time.

**Alternate Names:** *Whale's Tale*

**Variations on this Game**

- May be played head-to-head with the teams alternating when replaying the scenes.

# COUNTDOWN

(Start of the game) *"The players will play a 60-90 second setup scene, and I will be back to explain the rest in a moment."*

(After getting the style suggestions) *"Now the players will replay the scene in half of the time the original took."*

The referee gets a suggestion for the game, and the players begin with a neutral scene. After the scene is done, the referee will cut the time in half, forcing the scene to get faster. This happens multiple times, until the final scene is replayed in under five seconds.

# ELIMINATOR REPLAY

(Start of the game) *"The players will play a setup scene, and I will be back to explain the rest in a moment."*

(After getting the style suggestions) *"Now the players will replay the scene, but one of the players is now gone, and the others must fill in for them."*

The referee gets a suggestion for the game, and the players begin with a neutral scene. After the scene is done, the referee will have the audience choose a player at random to sit out. That player's character is filled in by the other players still in the game. This continues until there is only one player left.

**Alternate Names:** *Highlander, Half-Life*

# GROUNDHOG'S REPLAY

(Start of the game) *"The players will play a setup scene, and I will be back to explain the rest in a moment."*

(After getting the style suggestions) *"Now the players will replay the scene, but one player's character knows they have done the scene before."*

The referee gets a suggestion for the game, and the players begin with a neutral scene. After the scene is done, the referee will choose a player to be the Groundhog, who relives the scene. The first replay is the first time they have lived through it, the second time is a number less than 50, and the final time is any number at all. These numbers are provided by the audience.

# GROUNDHOG'S REPLAY

(Start of the game) *"The players will play a setup scene, and I will be back to explain the rest in a moment."*

(After getting the style suggestions) *"Now the players will replay the scene, but one player's character knows they have done the scene before."*

The referee gets a suggestion for the game, and the players begin with a neutral scene. After the scene is done, the referee will choose a player to be the Groundhog, who relives the scene. The first replay is the first time they have lived through it, the second time is a number less than 50, and the final time is any number at all. These numbers are provided by the audience.

# MULTIPLICITY

(Start of the game) *"One player will do a scene playing multiple characters, and I will be back to explain the rest in a moment."*

(After getting the style suggestions) *"Now we will add one player at a time to expand the scene, until all players are involved."*

The referee gets a suggestion for the game, and a single player begins with a simple fast scene with multiple characters, generally at least one for each player on their team. After the scene is done, the referee will have the audience choose a player at random to join in. They help the first player to expand the scene, a little more. This continues until all players are in aa fully fleshed out scene, playing their own characters.

# MULTIVERSE

(Start of the game) *"The players will play a short setup scene, and I will be back to explain the rest in a moment."*

(After getting the style suggestions) *"Now the players will replay the scene, but if different choice were made."*

The referee gets a suggestion for the game, and the players begin with a neutral scene. After the scene is done, the referee will have them replay it, but changing something in the scene, such as the location, an item used, or just a new choice being made based on suggestions from the audience for each replay.

**Alternate Names:** *Replay-cement*

**Variations on this Game**

• May be played with the referee calling "New Choice!" to a player early on in a replay, which will change the whole scene.

# NAIVE REPLAY

(Start of the game) *"One player will do a scene leaving breaks for other characters, and I will be back to explain the rest in a moment."*

(After getting the style suggestions) *"Now we will add one player at a time to expand the scene, until all players are involved."*

The referee sends all but one player out of the arena. The referee gets a suggestion for the game, and a single player will perform a full scene, leaving gaps for other players to fill in. The referee will then call in one player at a time, who will fill in the gaps in the scene. It is important the players do not change their actions, lines, or emotional response from replay to replay. The final player must fill in the rest of the gaps.

**Alternate Names and Variations:**

- May be played with only one player going out under the same name, and with all but one going out under the name (*Extreme Naive Replay*).

- May be played with a different genre mapped on top of each replay. (Called *Ultra Naive Replay*)

- May be played head-to-head with one player from each team staying in, and then alternating between players from each team joining in each replay. (Called *Mega Extreme Naive Replay*)

- May be played head-to-head, alternating between a player from each team joining in each replay. (Called *Mega Naive Replay*)

- May be played head-to-head, alternating between a player from each team joining in each replay, with a different genre mapped on top of each replay. (Called *Mega Ultra Naive Replay*)

# REPLAY AT BERNIE'S

(Start of the game) *"The players will play a setup scene, and I will be back to explain the rest in a moment."*

(After getting the style suggestions) *"Now the players will replay the scene, but one of the players is now dead, and the others must puppeteer their body."*

The referee gets a suggestion for the game, and the players begin with a neutral scene. After the scene is done, the referee will have the audience choose a player at random to "die." Their body is then puppeteered by the other players still in the game. This continues until there is only one player left.

**Variations on this Game**

- May be played with the number of dead bodies increasing every replay, but the referee switching who is dead and who is alive. (Called *Replay At Bernie's: Spinning Wheel of Death*)

# SKEWED

(Start of the game) *"The players will play a short setup scene, and I will be back to explain the rest in a moment."*

(After getting the style suggestions) *"Now the players will replay the scene, but from each of the players point of view."*

The referee gets a suggestion for the game, and the players begin with a neutral scene. After the scene is done, the referee will have them replay it from the viewpoint of each of the characters in the scene, or from other things points of view such as the announcer, an animal in the scene, etc.

**Alternate Names:** *Altered Viewpoints*

# TEMPORAL REPLAY

(Start of the game) *"The players will play a short setup scene, and I will be back to explain the rest in a moment."*

(After getting the style suggestions) *"Now the players will replay the scene in the different times."*

The referee gets a suggestion for the game, and the players begin with a neutral scene. After the scene is done, the referee will gather a list of three different time periods for the players to replay the scene in. They then replay in those time periods, changing the scene to match accordingly.

# GAMES NOT MENTIONED IN THIS SECTION

# JUSTIFICATION GAMES

Justification games are games in which a level of justifying your actions or words takes place. While some games lend themselves to you justifying them, in others it falls onto the shoulders of your teammates. Generally, a single team plays the justification games listed here, during the Team Choice/Team Challenge round.

# ACROMANIA

*"The players will play a scene where every so often an acronym will be said, and the players will explain its meaning."*

The referee gets a suggestion for the game, and the players begin playing a scene. Every so often, a player will use a multi-letter acronym in lieu of a word. Their teammate's next line will explain what that acronym stands for. As the game progress the acronyms become longer.

# DIME STORE NOVEL

*"One of the players will be writing a novel, while the other players will be acting it out."*

The referee gets a suggestion for the title of a novel that has never been written, and one player begins to write the novel aloud. While writing the novel, the author has overall control of the scene, while the other players will begin to fill out the rest of the novel, including the dialogue and actions. The focus of the scene should alternate back and forth regularly between author and players.

**Variations on this Game**

- May be played with a genre layered on top of the novel.

# INTERPRETER

*"The players will be on a talk show, with a foreign expert and their interpreter here to translate for them."*

The referee will get a suggestion of a fictional country and turn it over to the team. One player will serve as the host of the talk show, another will use gibberish to translate the question to the foreign expert, and the third and/or fourth players are foreign experts. The host will field questions from the audience, the interpreter will relay the question to the foreign expert(s) who will respond using physicality and gibberish, and then translate their answers into English.

**Variations on this Game**

- May be played with the host serving as the interpreter.

- May be played with one player as the host, one player as the gibberish expert, and one player translating it through pantomime. (Called *Interpretive Dance*)

# INSTANT SOAP OPERA

*"The players will do a soap opera inspired scene, where at any given time one player must be looking into the distance, one looking at another player, and the third splayed, without any player matching positions with another."*

The referee gets a suggestion for the game, and the players begin playing a soap opera inspired scene. The players must play the scene with the limitations of physical movements being one player must be looking out into the distance, one looking at another player, and the third splayed against the back wall or just in general. No two players may be in the same position at any given time, and the players must justify their movements between the positions.

**Variations on this Game**

- May be played with a fourth player, adding the position of biting their knuckle.

- May be played with the audience instructed to say "Oooohh" if two players are in the same position.

# LIMIT LINE

*"The players will do a scene where two players only have two lines of dialogue they are capable of saying, and the other may speak normally."*

The referee gets four lines of dialogue from the audience and assigns them to two of the players, gets a suggestion for the scene, and the players begin. One player is the neutral party, able to say whatever they wish in the scene, and it is this player's job to justify the other two players, who each can only say the two lines of dialogue given to them. Players with the limited lines may change the tone and emotionality with the delivery, but they must speak the lines only as given.

**Alternate Names:** *Two Lines*

# MEMENTO

*"The players will begin a scene at the very end, and whenever the lights go out and come back on we will see the scene immediately prior."*

The referee gets a suggestion, and the players begin a scene, which serves as the very end of a story. Whenever the lights turn off, and then back on, the players will do the scene that immediately preceded that one. The scenes will vary in length, and the process continues until the game is called to an end.

# OFFSTAGE DIRECTIONS

*"The players will begin a scene, and whenever the other team chooses, they may read a stage direction from a play, which will happen in the scene."*

The referee gets a suggestion, and the players begin a neutral scene. Whenever the other team chooses, they will read a stage direction from a random play, which the other team will immediately do and justify the action into the scene.

# OXYGEN DEPRIVATION (18+)

*"At any given time, a player will have their head submerged in a bucket of water, while their teammates perform a scene. When the player needs air, they will be tapped out by another player entering the water, and must justify being wet."*

A bucket of water is placed on the field and one player is chosen to go first. The referee gets a suggestion, the chosen player will submerge their head in the bucket, and the players begin a neutral scene. Whenever the player in the bucket needs air, they will raise and wave their hand. At this point one of their teammates will justify exiting the scene, tap out the player in need of air, and submerge their own head in the bucket. The wet player must justify their entrance, and their being wet.

**Variations on this Game**

- May be played with any fluid in the bucket.

# PAVLOVIAN RESPONSE

*"The players will begin a scene, and whenever their trigger happens, they must do their given reaction."*

The referee will instruct all of the players to turn their backs and cover their ears and hum. One by one the referee will bring a player forward to get a trigger how they will respond to said trigger. For example: "Whenever Player A takes three steps, the player must do what?" After all players are assigned a trigger and response, the referee will get a suggestion for the game, and the players will begin a neutral scene, only to respond when their trigger is done. They must justify this momentary response in the scene, and continue the scene. Actions taken in responses may trigger other players responses. As the game moves forward players try to figure out triggers and use them.

**Alternate Name:** *Rube Goldberg*

**Variations on this Game**

- May be played without the justification aspect of the game.

- May be played where actions done in responses do not trigger the other players response.

# PICK A PLAY

*"The players will begin a scene, however all but one player may only read lines from a play, while the other can speak normally."*

The referee will give all but one player scripts that they must use as their only lines of dialogue in the scene. The referee gets a suggestion, and the players begin a scene. The players with the script must only use the lines of dialogue from a chosen character in the play, shortening long monologues as needed, while the neutral player justifies their lines into the scene.

**Alternate Names:** *Actor's Nightmare; Scene on Book*

**Variations on this Game**

- May be played with a volunteer player as one of the players on book.

- May be played with only one player or volunteer player on book – this is what's typically called *Scene on Book*.

# PICK-UP LINES

*"The players will play a scene where every so often they will pick up a line of dialogue and read it, then justify it into the scene."*

The referee will send the players out of the room and get lines of dialogue from the audience, which the other team will write on slips of paper and place on the field. The referee calls the players back in, gets a suggestion for the game, and the players begin playing a scene. Every so often, a player will pick up a line of dialogue and immediately say it. This line of dialogue must be then justified into the scene.

**Alternate Names:** *Lines from the Audience*; formerly called *Blind Line*

**Variations on this Game**

- May be played where the lines picked up become the first line of a song. (Called *Pick-up Line Musical*)

- May be played where the referee gets stage directions as well as lines of dialogue. (Called *Stage Directions*)

- May be played with fortune cookies on the field in lieu of lines from the audience. (Called *Fortune Cookies*)

# REVOLVING DOORS

*"The players will play a scene where they will either enter or exit the scene whenever their given word is spoken."*

The referee assigns each player a word that might come up in casual conversation, gets a suggestion, and the players begin a neutral scene. Whenever another player in the scene speaks a player's word, that player must enter or exit. If the player's word is spoken and they are off the field, they must immediately come on field and justify their entrance. If their *word is spoken while on field they must immediately exit and* justify their exit.

**Alternate Names:** *Entrances and Exits*

# SIT STAND KNEEL LIE

*"The players will do a scene, where at any given time one player must be sitting, one must be standing, and the third player lying down, without any player matching positions another player."*

The referee gets a suggestion for the game, and the players begin playing a scene. The players must play the scene with the limitations of physical movements being one player must be sitting, one standing, and the third lying down. No two players may be in the same position at any given time, and the players must justify their movements between the positions.

**Variations on this Game**

- May be played with three players, removing the position of kneeling or lying.

- May be played with the audience instructed to say "Oooohh" if two players are in the same position.

# STAND BY SCENE

*"The players will play a scene, narrated by a voiceover of one player's future self."*

The referee gets a suggestion for the game, and the players begin playing a scene. Every so often a chosen player will provide a narration for one player, adding new information into the scene, as the narrator is that character's future self, à la *Stand by Me* or *The Wonder Years*.

**Variations on this Game**

- May be played with a volunteer player, with a player providing narration in the form of the volunteer player's future self.

- May be played with the announcer providing the single character's future selves narration.

# SUBTEXT

*"The players will begin a scene, however all but one player may only read texts from a volunteer player's phone, while the other can speak normally."*

The referee will get two random volunteer players unlocked cell phones, and give them to two players, they must use as their only lines of dialogue in the scene. The referee gets a suggestion, and the players begin a scene. The players with the cell phones must only use the lines of dialogue from side of the conversation in the texts, shortening longer ones as needed, while the neutral player justifies these lines into the scene.

**Alternate Names:** *Texts From Last Night*

**Variations on this Game**

• May be played with volunteer players texting the players' phones lines of dialogue they must use during the game, and played similar to *Pick-up Lines* (Called *Texts From Tonight*)

# UNCLE GIBBERISH

*"The players will play a scene; however, one player may only speak in gibberish, which the other players somehow are able to understand."*

The referee gets a suggestion for the game, and the players begin playing a scene. One player is chosen to only speak in gibberish, while the others will justify their gibberish when responding in English.

**Alternate Names:** *Aunt Gibberish; Uncle Vanya*

**Variations on this Game**

- May be played with a volunteer player as the gibberer.

- May be played with the referee switching between the players who is the one speaking gibberish (Called "*Uncle Gibberish Switch*")

- May be played with "I am Groot," "Hodor," or some other form of single word speaking pop culture figure. (Called whatever the pop culture character's name is.)

# GAMES NOT MENTIONED IN THIS SECTION

# VOLUNTEER PLAYER GAMES

Volunteer player games are one of the things that sets short-form or games-based improv apart from many other forms of comedy. While playing them, players should take care of the volunteer players by making them the star of the game through the referee coaching them through examples before any game begins, getting their consent when it comes to physical games, and treating them how you would like to be treated. Generally, a single team plays the volunteer player games listed here during the Team Choice/Team Challenge round. While most of these games may fall into other categories, as these games require a volunteer player component, they are found here.

# ARMS EXPERT (18 +)

*"We will get to interview an audience expert, but one player will be providing their arms."*

The referee asks for a volunteer player from the audience who is an expert in something, then the players begin a talk show style scene, where the expert's arms are those of a player standing behind them sticking their arms through the armholes of the expert, and another doing it for the interviewer.

**Alternate Names:** *Arms; Helping Hands*

**Variations on this Game**

- May be played without a volunteer player.
- May be played as normal scene, without the talk show genre.

**Warning**: Do not play this game without clear consent and clear boundaries from all participants.

# AUDIENCE SOUND EFFECTS

*"While the players play a scene, a volunteer player will provide all of the sound effects needed."*

The referee asks for a volunteer player from the audience, gets a suggestion for the game, and then the players begin a neutral scene. Whenever the players hear a sound effect they must justify it into the scene, and they may also prompt for specific sounds as well.

**Variations on this Game**

- May be played without a volunteer player.

- May be played with the volunteer player or sound person with their back turned, or in another room, so as they cannot see what is happening in the scene. (Called *Remote Sound Effects*)

# BEDTIME STORY

*"One player will be reading a volunteer player a bedtime story, but every so often the reader will ask for them to fill in a word."*

The referee asks for a volunteer player from the audience, gets a made-up title of a bedtime story. One player, the reader, begins to read the story to the volunteer player. Every so often, they will have the volunteer player fill in a word or part of the story. After some of the story has been told they will give focus to the offstage players, who will jump on the field and continue where the reader and volunteer player had left off. After the story has progressed a bit through the actions of the players, the reader will again take focus. This interchange repeats throughout.

**Variations on this Game**

- May be played with multiple volunteer players. (Called *Campfire Story*)

- The referee may get a genre for the story as well, and the name reflects that. (e.g. *Spooky Bedtime Story*)

# COFFEE BREAK

*"Our players will be working hard in the next scene, and whenever they need a break they will have a volunteer player take over their character until they come back."*

The referee asks for a volunteer player from the audience, gets a suggestion for the game, and the players begin a neutral scene. Whenever a player wishes, they may say "Coffee Break!" and the volunteer player will take over the player's character until the player returns.

# COLUMNS

*"The players will do a scene, however every so often they will be at a loss for words and the volunteer players will fill it in for them."*

The referee asks for two volunteer players from the audience, gets a suggestion for the game, and the players begin a neutral scene. The volunteer players are positioned on the corners of the field closest to the audience, and throughout the game the players will either tap their shoulder or look at them to fill in a word for them. The players will justify it, no matter what is said, as if they themselves said it.

**Alternate Names:** *Pillars*

**Variations on this Game**

- May be played with the volunteer players instead mouthing the words and the players attempting to read their lips. (Called *Teleprompter*)

- May be played with the whole audience, as opposed to just two volunteer players. (Called *Hesitation*)

# DAY IN THE LIFE

*"Our players will recreate a day in the life of one of our volunteer players, exactly how they perceived it to happen."*

The referee asks for a volunteer player who has had an interesting or special day recently, and interview them about it. The referee should get details such as names and descriptions of people involved, what they did in order throughout the day, etc. After the interview is done, if the players have any other questions, they may ask them before playing out the scene. The scene should encompass the volunteer player's day, with one player portraying the volunteer player and the rest of the team portraying everyone else.

**Variations on this Game**

- May be played head-to-head.

- May be played by interviewing a group of people.

- May layer a genre on top of the game, with the name being changed to reflect that. (e.g. *Day in the Life: Shakespeare*)

# DINNER AT JOE'S

*"The players will recreate an event where the volunteer player would be with friends and family, throughout which they will determine if the players actions is something they would actually do."*

The referee asks for a volunteer player and interview them about a family or friend gathering they have had recently, getting information about a few of the people that attended. After they describe each person, they will cast a player in that role, including casting themself. The team will begin to play a scene at the gathering, giving time for the volunteer player to "Ding" if they are acting correctly or "Buzz" if they are acting incorrectly after each offer. The bell and buzzer may be actual or players from the other team.

**Alternate Names:** *Family Dinner; Let's Get Together; Dinner With The Family*

**Variations on this Game**

- May be played head-to-head for a larger group.

- May get a suggestion of where the volunteer's friends and family would gather.

# DOUBLE SPEAK

*"The volunteer players will be joined at the hip with a player to form a single person and by speaking one word at a time."*

The referee asks for two volunteer players from the audience, gets a suggestion for the game, and then the players begin a neutral scene. The volunteer players are paired with players who will stand side by side to form a single character in the scene, speaking one word at a time. A third player is neutral in the scene.

# FOREIGN MOVIE

*"Tonight, we will get to see a new foreign film with a volunteer player and one player acting it out, and the others providing the subtitles."*

The referee asks for a volunteer player from the audience, gets a suggestion of the title of a foreign film never before seen. The volunteer player and a player act out the film in gibberish, while the other two players will translate their gibberish into English. While playing it should be one of the performers in the film gibbers, one player translates, the second performer in the film gibbers, and the second player translates. This continues.

**Alternate Names:** *Subtitles*

**Variations on this Game**

- When played with more than a team of three players, there will still only be two translators, with one of the translators translating two performers in the film.

- May be played without a volunteer player.

- May be played blind, with the translators' backs turned to the field as to not see the performers of the film.

# LAUGHTERHOUSE 5

*"The players will show what happens when one performer becomes unstuck in time and jumps around a volunteer player's most important life events."*

The referee interviews a volunteer player from the audience, and get information about three major life events in their life then chooses one as the starting point for the game, and the players begin playing out that life event. Whenever the referee wishes, they may interrupt the game and call out one of the other life events, and the players must justify their positions in that new event. The referee may also go to events previously visited and the scenes that had been established there must continue from the new positions.

# MOVING BODIES

*"The players will do a scene; however, they are only able to talk, and our volunteer players will have to move them around the field."*

The referee asks for a given number of volunteer players from the audience, gets a suggestion for the game, and the players begin a neutral scene. The volunteer players must move the players bodies throughout the space to do the scene, as the players are unable to do it themselves. This is accomplished by moving their arms, head, bend them over, etc. Walking is accomplished by tapping the back of the leg they want to move forward. Whenever the players are moved they must justify it into the scene, and they may also prompt for specific movements as well.

**Warning:** Please be clear with Volunteer Players about physical limits. Respect your team's boundaries if this game is discussed.

**Alternate Names:** *Human Puppets; Action Figures; Human Statues*

**Variations on this Game**

- May be played different ways to have players walk, be it simply touch the back, pushing forward, or even lifting their legs up.

- May be played without volunteer players, and the other team providing the moving of the bodies.

# NEWSCASTER

*"Our players will show how a day in the life of one of our volunteer player's day affects the whole world via a newscast."*

The referee asks for a volunteer player who has had an interesting or special day recently, and interview them about it. After the interview, the players begin to host a news show. One player takes the lead anchor position and will throw it to the other players to report on specific segments. These sections could be sports, economy, weather, etc., and they will map how they are affected by the special day.

**Variations on this Game**

- May be played head-to-head.

# SLIDE SHOW

*"The players and volunteer player are about to show us some slides from a recent trip, while another player tells us all about them."*

The referee asks for a given number of volunteer players from the audience, get a suggestion for a location, and the lights will go out on the field. While the lights are out, one of the players will begin to host a slide show of their recent trip to the suggested location, while the players and volunteer players pose for photos in the dark, freezing when the lights come on. The host will explain the photos to tell the story of the trip.

**Variations on this Game**

- May be played head-to-head.
- May have multiple hosts, if team size permits.

# SLO-MO

*"We are about to see the newest Olympic event. Our volunteer player and players will compete and provide the commentary."*

The referee asks for a volunteer player from the audience, get a suggestion of a mundane activity. The volunteer player and a player will begin to warm for the activity in regular speed, while they are introduced by the other two players acting as commentators. Once the announcer fires a starting pistol the two competitors switch to slow motion, while the commentators describe the action as if it were a high stakes sporting event.

**Alternate Names:** *Mundane Olympics; Everyday Olympics*

**Variations on this Game**

- May be played with more than one player and one volunteer player as competitors.

# TALK RADIO

*"One player will host a radio talk show interviewing a volunteer player, while the other players call in to the show with questions."*

The referee asks for a volunteer player from the audience who is an expert in something, then one player will introduce the radio show themed around the area of expertise. The host will get to know the volunteer player and their area of expertise for a bit before opening the phone lines for questions. The other players will be callers calling into the show, taking on characters with problems related to the area of expertise, and ask questions of the expert. The host helps to guide the volunteer player through the answers.

**Alternate Names:** *NPR; Talk of the Town*

**Variations on this Game**

- May be played head-to-head.

# THE EVENT

*"The players will show an event in the life of a volunteer player, as well as how history led up to and was changed by it."*

The referee asks for a volunteer player who has had an interesting or special event in their life recently, and interview them about it. After the interview, the players recreate the event in a short scene. One player will then interrupt the scene and give an amount of time before or after the event, phrased as "10 years before The Event!" or "20 minutes after The Event!" The players clear the field and we see that scene. One player plays the volunteer player throughout, if they are needed in any scenes.

**Variations on this Game**

- May be played head-to-head with the teams alternating between making the time jumps; only one player should play the main character. Ref should call the time jumps in this version.

# WHAT IF?

*"The players will show what would have happened if a volunteer player chose differently on a major decision, and how things would have changed."*

The referee asks for a volunteer player who has made a major life decision recently and interview them about it, then the players begin a scene where they play out what would have happened if the volunteer player chose differently. One player should play the volunteer player throughout. The team should good-naturedly show how bad things would have been, had the volunteer player chose the other path.

# WORD FROM OUR SPONSOR

*"One player will host a talk show interviewing a volunteer player, while the other players provide the commercials."*

The referee will ask for a volunteer player willing to be interviewed, and one player begins an interview style talk show with them. Throughout the interview, the host will use the responses as segues into commercial breaks using the line "Speaking of ___, here's a word from our sponsors." The other players will then do a commercial about whatever the host said.

**Variations on this Game**

- May be played with the referee getting three products, as opposed to using the segues from the interview.

- May be played with jingles instead of commercials.

# GAMES NOT MENTIONED IN THIS SECTION

# MUSICAL GAMES

Whether your team has canned music, karaoke tracks, an accompanist, or a full live orchestra, musical games are some of the most pleasing games for audiences, and some of the most intimidating games for players. But don't let that stop you from playing these games, just keep two things in mind: rhyming doesn't matter, and if you can't sing, sing louder. Generally, a single team plays the musical games listed here during the Team Choice/Team Challenge round. While most of these games may fall into other categories, as these games generally require a heavy musical component, they can be found here.

Games that are musical variations on games previously mentioned can be found by name in the index, or by looking for the similar game. For example: *Tony Winning Moment* can be found with *Oscar Winning Moment*.

# AUDIENCE & HAMMERSTEIN

*"Based on your suggestions of three unrelated song titles, the players will perform a new, never before seen musical."*

The referee gets the suggestions of three unrelated made up song titles, and the name of a never before produced musical, the players then begin a scene in the style of musical comedy. As they play they will attempt to seamlessly work the three songs into the scene.

**Variations on this Game**

- May be played with the title of the song being the chorus, so that the audience may sing along. (Called *Audience Sing Along*)

# BLANK! THE MUSICAL

*"Every movie is getting turned into a musical these days, and tonight our players will turn another film into one."*

The referee gets the suggestion of a film which has not been turned into a musical, asking for more information about the movie if it is obscure. The players will then perform a scene turning that movie into a musical.

**Variations on this Game**

- May be played with a fairy tale, historic event, or other existing property.

# GIBBERISH OPERA

*"The team will perform for you a new never before seen opera in gibberish, but don't worry a helpful narrator will help explain what's happening."*

The referee gets the title of a made-up opera, and one player steps forward to serve as the narrator. The narrator will introduce the title of the opera, and pimp the players with a bit of exposition for the first act. The players perform the first act in gibberish, then the narrator comes back again to explain what happened, and set up the players for a second act. Repeat for act three, when all of the performers are married or dead.

**Variations on this Game**

- May be played with a volunteer player.

# IPSO FACTO OPERA

(Start of the game) *"The players will perform an opera for you in gibberish, then I will back to explain the rest in a moment."*

(After the gibberish opera) *"And now they will replay that opera for you in English, but with a totally new suggestion."*

The referee gets a suggestion, and the players begin to perform an opera in gibberish about it. Once they have finished the opera, the referee will get a new suggestion and have them replay the opera, but this time in English and about the new suggestion. Players should try to match the actions and emotions as the gibberish one, justifying them into the new opera.

**Variations on this Game**

- May be played head-to-head, with one team performing the gibberish opera, and the other performing the English version. They then switch.

# LOUNGE LIZARDS

*"The host of our night club will lead a variety of performers to serenade our volunteer player."*

The referee asks for a volunteer player from the audience, and a player then begins to interview the volunteer player as if they are a guest at a fancy old fashioned night club. Throughout the interview the host will find segues into letting the volunteer player know they have a performer here to sing a song about their responses. The host introduces the performer, and the performer sings the song to the volunteer. This repeats until all players have sung.

**Variations on this Game**

- May be played with the host singing a closing number, bringing together all the performers once more.

# MADRIGAL

*"The players will perform a newly discovered 16th century madrigal, which I will conduct."*

The referee has the players line up, getting a multi-word suggestion for each of them. These suggestions are generally tabloid headlines, pieces of advice, advertising slogans, etc. After the players each have their suggestion, the referee will begin to conduct them, each singing their suggestion two or four times by themselves. After a player has sung their line, they will sing a couple of the syllables in rhythm, supporting the rest of the players. Once all players have sung once, they will begin to change their suggestion by mixing in words from the other singers, subtly at first, and more so as the game progress. During the third time through the referee will designate one of the player's mixed up line as the ending chorus, and all players join in singing that new line in unison.

**Variations on this Game**

- May be played with players singing all of their lines loudly, at the same time, in between each time through.

- May be played in the style of rapping, going once through with the lines as suggested, mixed up the second time through, and free flow rapping about the subjects mentioned on the third. (Called *Rap Madrigal*)

# MUSICAL GENRE

*"The players will perform a scene in the style of (genre)"*

The referee gets a suggestion, and the players begin performing a scene in whatever style they have chosen. **This game is not called Musical Genre**. It is called whatever genre the team had selected to do the scene in (Musical Comedy, Opera, Rock Opera, Blues Jam, A Capella Jam, etc.).

**Alternate Names:** Many, again it is dependent upon the genre of musical the team is performing in.

**Variations on this Game**

- May be played head-to-head

# PIANO TORTURE

*"The players will be doing a scene, but whenever the accompanist wishes they can begin playing, and the players must begin singing, and stop whenever the music stops."*

The referee gets a suggestion for the game, and the players begin with a neutral scene. Whenever the accompanist wishes, they will play music and the players must immediately switch from speaking talking to singing, and back to talking when the music stopped, never addressing the change.

# SCHOOLHOUSE MOCK

*"The players will solve a problem with the help of a mysterious stranger in the style of Schoolhouse Rock."*

The referee gets the suggestion of a common problem or concept, and two players begin a scene where they are children not understanding the suggestion. The third player enters as a character themed around the suggestion and teaches the kids about it through song, a la Schoolhouse Rock. The kids join in, but bring up something else tied to the suggestion, which the third player also teaches them about. The game ends with all the players singing about what they have learned.

### Variations on this Game

May be played with four players, with the fourth coming in as a second character to teach about the second concept.

# SHAM-ILTON

*"To capitalize on the success of Hamilton, our players will create a new hit rap musical about another historical figure."*

The referee gets a suggestion of a historical figure, and asks the audience for a little information about the historical figure if it is an obscure one, then the players perform a musical about the historical figure, entirely through rap.

# SING IT

*"The players will begin a scene, and throughout it I can blow my whistle and call for a specific player to 'Sing It!' and they will sing a song based on their last line of dialogue."*

The referee gets a suggestion for the game, and the players begin with a neutral scene. Whenever the referee wishes, they may interrupt the game and call out a player, and line of dialogue, then encourage the audience to join them in declaring "Sing it!". That player will begin to sing a song based on that line, generally with the line becoming the chorus. During their song, the other players may join in for back up, or to move the song forward. The player, referee, or musician can end the song.

**Variations on this Game**

- May be played with rapping instead of singing, with the referee declaring "Kick it!" (Called *Kick It*)

- May be played with the songs being super short, and straight to the point, about two lines. (Called *No Time For Musicals*)

# THAT SOUNDS LIKE A SONG

*"The players will begin a scene, and throughout it, if a player hears something they like they can let the other player know that 'That sounds like a song.' Their teammate will then break into a musical number."*

The referee gets a suggestion for the game, and the players begin with a neutral scene. Whenever a player hears a line of dialogue from their teammate that they like, they may say to them that their offer "Sounds like a song." After this is said the player who spoke will sing a song based on their last line of dialogue generally with the line becoming the chorus. During their song, the other players may join in for back up, or to move the song forward. The player, referee, or musician can end the song.

**Variations on this Game**

- May be played with rapping instead of singing, with the player declaring "That gets a bad rap!" (Called *That Gets a Bad Rap*)

# THREE-HEADED BROADWAY STAR

*"The players will serenade you all, by singing a song one word at a time."*

The referee gets a suggestion for a song, and the players line up side by side. They begin singing the song one word at a time.

**Variations on this Game**

• May be played with a volunteer player, whom the referee has interviewed. The players sing the song to them.

# TIN PAN ALLEY

*"One of the players will treat us as investors, setting the scene for songs from their new musical."*

The referee gets a suggestion for the name of a musical that has never been produced, and one player will step onto the field as if entering a pitch room. They begin to tell everyone about the musical, setting up the scenes and songs. When the pitchperson is done, the remaining players will perform the aforementioned scene and song.

**Variations on this Game**

May be played head-to-head with one player from each team working together to pitch the show.

# GAMES NOT MENTIONED IN THIS SECTION

# CATCH-ALL GAMES

Catch-all games are games in a category all of their own. Some of these games are considered "hoop" games, as they force the players to jump through hoops to complete them. Others just are difficult to choose one significant category for them to fall into. Generally, the catch-all games listed here are played by a single team during the Team Choice/Team Challenge round.

# AB SCENE

*"The players will play a scene where every line of dialogue must begin with the next letter of the alphabet."*

The referee gets a suggestion for the game, and the players begin playing a scene. Each line of dialogue must begin with the next letter of the English alphabet.

**Alternate Names:** ABC Scene

**Variations on this Game**

- May be played where the referee gets a random letter of the alphabet to begin on.

- May be played with the lines of dialogue starting with the preceding letter of the alphabet, making the alphabet backwards.

# ACRONYM PANEL

*"We have gathered together a panel of experts to share what different acronyms mean in their field."*

The players stand in a line, and step forward one by one introducing themselves in character. The referee gets a suggestion of an acronym from the audience, and one by one, each player explains what that acronym means to them. The process repeats until the referee ends the game.

**Variations on this Game**

- May be played with the referee suggestions for the players' characters on the panel.

# ADVICE PANEL

*"We have gathered together a panel of experts to share their advice for your questions."*

The players stand in a line, and step forward one by one introducing themselves in character. The referee asks if anyone in the audience needs advice about something, and has an audience member ask their question. One by one, each player offers advice to them. The process repeats until the referee ends the game.

**Variations on this Game**

- May be played with the referee suggestions for the players' characters on the panel.

- May be played where one player always give good advice, one always gives bad, and one gives the worst or another endowment (Called *Good, Bad, Worst Advice* or *Good, Bad, ___ Advice* depending on the endowment.)

- May be played where the referee gets questions about anything, and the panel answers the questions. (Called *Expert Panel*)

# ALPHABET GENRE

*"The players will do a scene in a brand-new genre."*

The referee gets a letter from the audience, and each player gives a suggestion of a new made up genre that starts with that letter. The audience votes for which genre the want to see, and the players do a scene in that genre.

**Variations on this Game**

- May be played head-to-head.

- Some cities get multiple letters that make for a multi-word genre.

- Some cities make a whole list of genres starting with the letter and play it similar to "Changing Styles."

# BUZZFEED

*"Just like on Buzzfeed does with everything else, our players will share the top ten scenes about your suggestion.*

The referee gets a suggestion, and the players begin a quick neutral scene. The players then do nine more based on the same suggestion.

**Variations on this Game**

- May be played head-to-head.

- May be played with however many scenes the referee wishes to assign the team.

# CRITIC

*"The players will review and show us a few clips from upcoming films."*

The referee will get the suggestions of two made up movie titles, and two genres. One or two players take on the role of a movie critic, and introduce the film and its genre, and a little bit about the plot, then the rest of the team acts out a quick scene from that movie. The critics will then talk about another scene, challenging the players with a plot point, cameo, etc., and the rest of the team acts out a second scene. This repeats for the second movie title and genre.

**Alternate Names:** *Movie Critic; Movie Review; At The Movies*

**Variations on this Game**

- May be played head-to-head with one review from each team, and the other players working together.

- May be played with other mediums, such as television, video games, theater, etc. (Called "___ Review" dependent on the medium chosen."

# DR. KNOW-IT-ALL

*"The world-famous Dr. Know-It-All is here to answer all of your questions, albeit one word at a time."*

The players stand shoulder-to-shoulder, or with their arms around each other, and introduce themself as Dr. Know-It-All, speaking one word at a time. The referee asks if anyone in the audience a question about anything, and has an audience member ask their question. The players answer one word at a time, in the first person. The process repeats until the referee ends the game.

**Variations on this Game**

- May be played with a volunteer player.

- May be played with the players lined up like a totem pole, ending each answer with a spooky "Oooohhh," or with the phrase "The Oracle Has Spoken. Oooohhh." Waving their arms spookily. This variation may also be played with an audience member. (Called *Oracle*)

- May be played with all the players attempting to speak in unison as opposed to one word at a time. (Called *Dr. Share-A-Tongue*)

- May be played head-to-head with each team being either Dr. Know-It-All or Dr. Share-A-Tongue, and debating a topic from the audience. (Called *Dr. Debate*)

# DUBBING

*"The players will be playing a scene, but other players will be providing their voices, instead of them providing their own."*

The referee gets a suggestion and two players begin a scene, with players off-field dubbing the players on the field, who move their mouths and play out the scene.

**Variations on this Game**

- May be played with a volunteer player.

- May be played with the dubbers in another room, or with their backs turned to the field. (Called *Remote Dubbing*)

- May be played with all players playing the scene with Player A dubbing Player B, Player B dubbing Player C, and Player C dubbing Player A. (Called *Three-Way Dubbing*)

# EMOTIONAL ROLLERCOASTER

*"Each player will have a strong emotion, that whenever they enter the scene overtakes everyone."*

The referee will get suggestions of emotions and assign one to each of the players. One player begins a one-person scene, and as the players enter one by one, every player takes on the emotional state of the newly entered player. Players leave in reverse order, taking their emotion with them, until the original player is alone again.

**Alternate Names:** *Emotional Party*

**Variations on this Game**

• May be played with genres, voices, or any other type of endowment the referee wishes to assign. (Called "Chameleon")

# EMOTIONAL SYMPHONY

*"I will be conducting the players through a symphony where emotions are the instruments."*

The referee gets a suggestion of an emotion for each of the players, who then line up shoulder to shoulder. The referee will then conduct them through a symphony, where when they point at a player the make noises associated with the emotion giving to them.

Emotional Symphony can be used as a match-ending tribute to the fans, and is effective on Road Shows.

**Variations on this Game**

- May be played with animal noises instead of emotions. (Called *Barnyard Symphony*)

- May be played using other endowments other than emotions, such as facial expressions in IDs, ages, celebrities, etc. (Called "___ Symphony" dependent upon the endowments used)

# FINISHING SCHOOL

*"The players will do a scene with perfect posture, and if their posture fails, they must start again from the beginning."*

The referee gets a suggestion for the game and the players begin to perform a scene while balancing books on their heads. If at any point the books fall off, the players must start the scene again from the beginning.

# FLASH PHRASE

*"The players will morph common phrases, and then do a series of scenes based on the new phrases."*

The players line up on the field, and the referee gets a suggestion of a common phrase or idiom. One by one the players will subtly change the wording of the phrase until the referee hears one they like. This becomes the suggestion for a scene. During the scene, the referee may interrupt the scene, repeat the last line of dialogue and the players will subtly change it, like they had done at the beginning of the game, until the referee again hears one they like. This process repeats.

**Variations on this Game**

- May be played with the referee getting a new phrase or idiom each time they want to see a new scene.

# GAME-O-MATIC

*"The players will each pitch a new game and we will vote on which one we want to see played."*

The referee gets a suggestion of any two words, this becomes the name of a new game. The players will then pitch their idea on how the game is played, and the audience will vote on which they want to see. If the referee needs any clarification, they will ask for it from the player. The referee gets a suggestion for the game, and the players play it.

Special Note: The game that is created can be a completely new game, a twist on an existing one, or just "Forward Reverse."

**Variations on this Game**

- May be played with the referee getting initials and the names of the game are created similarly to *Alphabet Genre*.

- May be played head-to-head with each team inventing a new game for the other to play.

# GENRE PIECE

*"The players will perform a scene in the style of (genre)"*

The referee gets a suggestion, and the players begin performing a scene in whatever style they have chosen. **This game is not called Genre Piece**. It is called whatever genre the team had selected to do the scene in (Shakespeare, Afterschool Special, Noir, Teen Drama, etc.).

**Alternate Names:** Many, again it is dependent upon the genre the team is performing in.

**Variations on this Game**

- May be played head-to-head.

# IF *BLANKS* RULED THE WORLD

*"The players will show us some alternate worlds where different people are in charge of different things."*

The referee will get a list of three people or groups, and a list of three occasions, jobs, or locations. The players will then perform three scenes, showing what it would be like if that group or person ran the location, job, or occasion.

**Alternate Names:** It Could Happen

**Variations on this Game**

- May be played head-to-head, with four suggestions of each, and each team performing two scenes.

- May be played with only celebrities and occupations. (Called *Career Fair*)

# MARSHMALLOW (18+)

*"The players will perform a dramatic scene, and if whenever they make you laugh they will have to put a marshmallow in their mouth for the remainder of the scene."*

The referee gets a suggestion for the game, and the players begin a neutral scene. If at any point the audience truly laughs, the ref will call on that player to put a marshmallow in their mouth. The players cannot chew or swallow it until the game is over.

**Alternate Names:** *Chubby Bunny; Peeps*

**Variations on this Game**

- May be played with any food, such as bananas, hot mustard, Peeps, etc. (Called "____" dependent upon the food used.)

- May be layered on to any game. (Called *Marshmallow* ____ dependent upon the game it is layered upon.)

**Warning**: make sure all players know the risks with this game, and allow players to opt out.

# MOUSETRAP (18+)

*"The players will perform a scene; however, they are barefoot, blindfolded, and there are mousetraps on the field."*

The referee will get a suggestion for the game, and the players begin a neutral scene. The players are also all barefoot, blindfolded, and the field is covered in readied mousetraps.

**Warning**: make sure all players know the risks with this game, and allow players to opt out.

# MUNDANE ZOMBIE ATTACK

*"The players will play a scene, but throughout it they will dispatch zombies that invade their scene."*

The referee will get a suggestion for the game, and the players begin a neutral scene. Throughout the scene, the players from the other team will invade the scene as zombies. The team playing will use items found in their scene's location to inadvertently dispose of the zombies, ignoring their presence.

**Variations on this Game**

• May be played with the acknowledging the zombies, but treating them only as a nuisance.

# MY MOVIE

*"The players will pitch some new movie titles, and if I like the title, they will tell us more about it. If I like what I hear, we will see a scene from it."*

The referee gets a suggestion for the game, and the players line up shoulder to shoulder on the field. In unison, the players will say "My Movie! My Movie! My Movie!" Whenever the referee points at a player they will pitch a title themed around the suggestion, and if the referee wants to hear more they will let the player know. The player then gives the genre of the film, followed by a one sentence premise, and if the referee likes it they will get the audience to all say, "Let's see it!" The players then perform a quick scene from the film. This process repeats when the referee gets a new suggestion.

**Variations on this Game**

- May be played with the referee getting a letter in lieu of a suggestion, and all titles start with that letter.

- May be played with television series instead of films. (Called *New Fall Line Up*)

- May be played with songs instead of films. (Called *My Songy or Top Charts*)

- May be played with the referee getting a suggestion of a topic, which when pointed at the players will say a fact about. If the referee likes a fact the players perform a scene about that fact. (Called *Factfinder*)

- May be played head-to-head.

# NO SEE, NO HEAR, NO SPEAK

*"The players will perform a scene; however, one player will be blindfolded, one cannot speak, and one will not be listening to any of the other players."*

The referee will get a suggestion for the game, and the players will begin a neutral scene, however one player will be blindfolded or have their eyes closed, one player will not speak or have tape over their mouth, and the third will act as though they can't hear any of the other players or have in noise cancelling headphones.

- May be played with other mediums such as literature, television, theater, etc.

# REMAKE

*"With every movie getting remade these days, we will remake another one for you tonight."*

The referee gets the suggestion of a film, asking for more information if the film is obscure and a genre, and the players will begin to do a scene remaking the film, but in the new genre.

**Alternate Names:** *Reboot*

# SEARS FAMILY PORTRAIT

*"The players will be posing for a family photo, but not all families are as happy as the photos might make it seem."*

The referee will get a suggestion of an event, while the players assemble in a pose for a family portrait. The players cannot move, but discuss the event, raising the emotional stakes while attempting to stay in a pose for the camera.

**Variations on this Game**

- May be played with the name of a club from high school instead of a family picture. (Called "Yearbook")

- May be played head-to-head.

# SPELLING BEE

*"The players just came in second place at the national spelling bee, and will now show off spelling words for you, one letter at a time."*

The players line up on the field shoulder to shoulder, and the referee will get the suggestion of a simple word. The players will say the word in unison, spell one letter at a time as fast as they can, then repeat the word. After the word is spelled, the referee will have them use it in a sentence, the players will again repeat the word, speak the sentence one word at a time, and once more, repeat the word. This continues and repeats with the referee getting increasingly difficult words. Rather than having the players use the word in a sentence each time, the referee may ask them to define it, give country of origin, synonyms of the word, or anything else they choose. If a word is spelled incorrectly, the players will not acknowledge it and keep going.

**Variations on this Game**

- May be played with a volunteer player.

# SPORK RIVER

*"The players will share stories of the characters and the relationships in a small town."*

The referee will get the name of a made-up town. One by one the players will step on the field introduce themselves, and give a little information about the town and its residents, the freeze in pose. After all players have gone, one at a time the players will unfreeze, telling more of the story of the town's residents, then freezing again. No players may be unfrozen or talking at the same time.

**Alternate Names:** *Spoon River; Our Town*

**Variations on this Game**

- May be played head-to-head.

- May be played with the suggestion of an event instead of a location.

- May be played with this being the story of how players all died, once they die in the story the players lie down dead for the rest of the game.

# STUDIO AUDIENCE

*"The players will perform a scene before a live studio audience."*

The referee sections off the audience into three sections, each will have a specific job when they are pointed at. One section will laugh when pointed at, another will applaud and cheer, and the third will say "Aaawww". The referee then gets a suggestion for the game and the players begin a neutral scene. Whenever the players want to, the will point to a section of the audience, and they will respond appropriately.

**Variations on this Game**

- May be played with the referee or a volunteer player conducting the audience's response.

# SUPERHERO EULOGY

*"A true hero has died, and to speak tonight we have brought some of their closest friends and family."*

The referee will get the suggestion of a made-up superhero, and the players begin to grieve as if at a wake. One by one, the players will step to the front of the field, introduce themself, connection to the hero, and share a story. The characters can be sidekicks, partners, the mayor, a villain, etc.

**Variations on this Game**

- May be played with an existing fictional character. (Called *Fictional Eulogy*)

- May be played head-to-head.

# TAKE MY PANTS

(Start of the game) *"The players will play a setup scene, and I will be back to explain the rest in a moment."*

(After getting the style suggestions) *"Now the players will replay the scene, but one player's character knows they have done the scene before."*

The referee gets a suggestion for the game, and the players begin with a neutral scene. After the scene is done, the referee will choose a player to be the Groundhog, who relives the scene. The first replay is the first time they have lived through it, the second time is a number less than 50, and the final time is any number at all. These numbers are provided by the audience.

**Alternate Names:** *Groundhog's Replay*

# TOOTS MCGOOTS

*"The players will be performing and scene, and every so often there will be a fart noise. Whenever a player begins to laugh, one of their teammates will rotate in."*

The referee gets a suggestion for the game, and two players begin a very serious scene. Whenever the announcer wants they will make a fart noise, during which the players must stop speaking and allow tension to build. Whenever a player begins to laugh, a new player assumes their role. If they do not laugh, play continues as if nothing happened.

**Alternate Names:** *The Fart Game*

**Variations on this Game**

- May be played head-to-head, with one player from each team starting the scene.

# GAMES NOT MENTIONED IN THIS SECTION

# GUESSING GAMES

All improvisers know how to do scene work, can play most of the other games in this book, and will probably look great playing them. Guessing games, however, are a different beast, they are some of the most challenging games, but each match is greatly improved by the addition of one. Generally, the guessing games listed here are played by a single team during the Go Ahead/ Catch-Up round, but may be played in the Team Choice/Team Challenge rounds as well.

# ANIMATRONIC JAMBOREE

*"The players will perform an animatronic version of your suggestion, and the guesser will have to correctly identify the suggestion and the moving parts."*

The referee sends one player out of the room to be the guesser and gets the suggestion of a historical event, fairy tale, movie, etc. The team, along with the other team's players, each pick an item from that event and form an animatronic Chuck-E-Cheese band-esque tableau of the suggestion. The referee will ask each player what they are in the tableau, then the players all "power down" by bending over slack.

The referee will call the guesser back in, and "power up" the full tableau, with the players moving statically to tell the story of the suggestion as if animatronic robots. After a moment or two, the referee will "power down" the animatrons, and the guesser attempts to guess what they are seeing. If the guesser gets it right they move on, if they get it wrong the referee will tell them what it was. The referee will then "power up" an individual or group of animatrons to perform their part of the tableau, for the guesser to guess each player's individual part. Whether right or wrong, once the guesser guesses what a player is, the leave the field. This continues until all animatrons are guessed.

**Variations on this Game**

- May be played with a volunteer player.

- May be played head-to-head with either a volunteer player as the guesser, the guesser taking turns as to who guess first, or a guesser from each team writing their guesses down.

# BLITZ

*"The guesser will be put into an array of stories, and need to guess what stories they are in."*

The referee sends one player out of the room to be the guesser and gets a list of nine or more stories, video games, movies, plays, television shows, etc. The referee calls the guesser back in, and sets a timer for three minutes. Using only pantomime and gibberish the guesser's teammates will put them in the stories, in the order that they were suggested. Once the guesser believes they know it, they will step forward and guess. Right or wrong the team moves on to the next item on the list. This continues until either all items are guessed or time runs out, whichever comes first. The guesser then gives a final guess.

# CHAIN MURDER

*"There has been a murder, and our players will have to figure out where the murder took place, who was murdered, and with what weapon."*

The referee sends all but one player out of the room to guess, the remaining player will be the first cluegiver. They then get a suggestion of a location, occupation, and an unlikely murder weapon. The referee then calls in one of the guessers, and starts a timer for three minutes.

Through pantomime and gibberish, the cluegiver must get across the location, occupation, and weapon in that order. Once the guesser believes they know what the weapon is, they will use it to kill the cluegiver, and the timer stops. The referee calls in the next guesser, starts the timer again where it left off, and the new cluegiver tries to relay the information to the new guesser in a new way. This continues until all guessers have been giving the information or time runs out, whichever comes first. The players then will line up in order from first cluegiver to last player to guess. The last player in the room tries to guess the location. If they guess incorrectly the referee gives the second to last player in the room a chance, and so on, until someone gets it right or the first cluegiver tells them what it was. This process repeats for the occupation and the weapon.

**Variations on this Game**

- May be played with a volunteer player as the final guesser.

- May be played with the suggestions of where you had lunch, who you had lunch with, and what was in your sandwich. (Called *Lunch Break*)

# CRYSTAL BALL

*"A player will have to guess a teammates future, using only clues from them and their crystal ball."*

The referee sends one player out of the room to be the guesser, and then gets a suggestion of a celebrity or fictional character, a secret that person has, and how they will fall in love. The guesser is called back into the room, and a timer is set for three minutes.

The guesser takes on the character of a psychic. With the help of one teammate playing the client giving inference clues, and another teammate playing the crystal ball giving pantomime clues, the psychic must guess who the client will fall in love with. Once the psychic has correctly guessed this, the team moves on to the secret, and finally the way they fall in love. All guessing must be made before the time runs out, no final guessing.

**Variations on this Game**

- May be played with how the client will die instead of fall in love.

- May be played with four players, with two players acting as the crystal ball.

# DATING GAME

*"One lucky player will be sent on a date with one of these fine contestants, only they don't know who the contestants are."*

The referee sends one player out of the room to be the guesser, and gets a suggestion of an endowment for each player, now a contestant on a dating game style show. These might be a fictional character, celebrity, historical figure, appliance, animal, whatever the referee wants, and assigns them to the contestants. The referee calls in the guesser, who will endow themselves as a character looking for a date, and interviews them.

The contestants introduce themselves, without saying exactly who or what they are, and the guesser asks their first question to the contestants. Each contest will answer in character giving subtle inference clues as to who or what they are. This happens two more times. Once three questions have been asked of the contestants, the guesser will eliminate two contestants by guessing their endowment, and right or wrong the leave the field. Finally, the guesser declares they will be going on a date with the last contestant standing, and guess their endowment, right or wrong they exit the field together.

**Variations on this Game**

- May be played with each contestant having two endowments. (Called *Double Dating Game*)

# FIVE THINGS

*"The team will try to get their guesser to do five activities, with the changes to the activities, using only pantomime and gibberish in a set amount of time."*

The referee sends one player out of the room to be the guesser and gets suggestions of five activities. After getting the activities, the referee will replace the items used in said activity with other suggestion, getting two or three changes per activity. The remaining players will select what order they are doing the activities in, and the guesser is called back in, and a timer is set for four-five minutes.

Using only pantomime and gibberish, the players will attempt to get the guesser to do the activity. It is important to repeat the players giving clues do not do the activity. Once the guesser does the activity, the players will begin to show the changes by removing the object and replacing it with the suggested changes. Once the guesser believes they know it, they will do the activity with the changes. The referee then asks them to step forward and guess what they are doing and the changes. If the guesser gets it right, they move on to the next activity. If the guesser gets it wrong, their team will choose to fix it, or move on to the next and come back to it later if time allows. This repeats until time runs out or all activities are guessed correctly, whichever comes first. The guesser then gives a final guess.

**Variations on this Game**

- May be played with all players going out of the room, so the players giving clues don't see the list until the start of the game. (Called *Extreme Five Things*)

- May be played with all of the players going out of the room, and the activities and changes on separate slips of paper, with the guesser switching out between the activities. (Called *Ultra Extreme Five Things*)

- May be played with the referee getting the suggestion of a movie, and activities from said movie. The game is played as normal, but the guesser can get a bonus if the also can identify the film. (Called *Movie Five Things*)

- May be played with the first activity having only one change, the second activity having two changes, and so on until the fifth activity having five changes. (Called *1-2-3-4-5 Things*)

- May be played head-to-head with one guesser from each team leaving the room. The referee getting four or six activities and changes, and an optional seventh to serve as a tiebreaker. The teams taking one-minute turns to get their guesser to guess an activity, if their guesser fails to guess it correctly, the guesser from the other team gets a chance to steal. The tiebreaker is done by both team simultaneously, with the first guesser to step forward and get it right winning the point. (Called *Four Things* and *Six Things* respectively)

# HOSTAGE NEGOTIATOR

*"A player has taken a player hostage, and won't them go until they find out where they are, what weapon they are using, and what they want."*

The referee sends one player out of the room to be the guesser, and then gets a suggestion of a location, an unlikely weapon, and a ridiculous demand. The guesser is called back into the room and a timer is set for three minutes. The guesser takes on the character of a hostage taker, with one player as the hostage, and another as the negotiator. Through increasingly less subtle inference clues, they will try to get the guesser to guess where they are. Once they do the team moves on to the weapon and the demand. The game ends when the guesser correctly guess the demand, or time runs out, whichever comes first.

**Alternate Names:** *Negotiator*

**Variations on this Game**

- May be played as a child planning a party with the suggestions of where the party is, what gift they want, and what activity the will be doing. (Called *Sweet Sixteen*)

- May be played as a player planning a wedding with the suggestions of where the wedding is, what their dress is made out of, and what food they will have. (Called *Wedding Planner*)

- May be played with a sports coach giving a pep talk with the suggestions of the activity, a mascot, and the famous person in the crowd. (Called *Pep Talk*)

- May be played with a spokesperson giving a press conference with the suggestion of what happened, where it happened, and what the effect will be. (Called *Press Conference*)

# HOT BELL

*"Speaking one word at a time, the team will try to get a guesser to guess your suggestion."*

The referee sends the whole team out of the room, and gets a list of seven or more suggestions. The referee then calls the players back in and sets a timer for three minutes.

One player starts as a guesser, and their teammates will try to get them to guess the suggestion speaking one word at a time, and then dinging a bell when they are done. The guesser makes a guess and right or wrong the team rotates in a new guesser. This continues until all suggestions are guessed, or time runs out. No final guesses are given.

**Variations on this Game**

- May be played with a volunteer player as the guesser the whole time.

- May be played head-to-head with teams taking turns giving clues and guessing. If the team gets it wrong a guesser from the other team can steal.

# INTERROGATION

*"One player has committed a crime, only they don't know what the crime was, why they did it, or who they were with. Luckily, the cops interrogating them do."*

One player is sent out of the room to be the guesser, and the referee gets the suggestion of an activity that is not a crime, an unrelated motive, and an accomplice. The guesser is called back in and a timer is set for three minutes.

The guesser takes on the character of a culprit, with the other players as detectives. Through increasingly less subtle inference clues, they will try to get the culprit to guess what they did. Once they culprit confesses to the crime, they will move on to the motive, and the accomplice. It must all be guessed before the timer is done. There are no final guesses.

**Alternate Names:** *Crime Story*

**Variations on this Game**

- May be played with the culprit as some in the principal's office, at home with their parents, or at the location of any authority figure for that manner – *Late For Curfew; Principal's Office*, etc

- May be played with four players, with the fourth player being a second culprit in a separate room.

# LIE DETECTOR

*"One team is perfect at detecting when lines are scripted, and will be able to point them out in a scene performed by the other team."*

One team is sent out of the room to be the guessers, and the referee will get five lines of dialogue from the audience. The guessing team is called back in, and a timer is set for three minutes.

The guessing team lines up off field in a straight line, and the opposing team begins to perform a scene, trying to work in the scripted lines of dialogue into it. Whenever the player at the front of the guessing team thinks a line is scripted they will declare "That's a line!" If they are correct, they stay at the front of the line, if they are incorrect the go to the back of the line and a new guesser will step forward. If a line of dialogue sneaks past the guessers, the referee announces it. This continues until all lines are used or time runs out, whichever comes first.

**Variations on this Game**

- May be played with the referee getting only statements of fact.

- May be played with the players declaring "That's a line!" instead of "That's a lie!" (Called "Line Detector")

# MYSTERY WHERE

*"The team will do a scene, but each player believes they are in a different location."*

The referee sends the whole team out of the room, and gets a suggestion of location for each player. The referee calls back in the team, which lines up away from the field. One by one the referee whispers a location to each player, and the players go to separate parts of the field. A timer is set for three minutes.

The referee gets a suggestion for the game, and the players begin to play a scene, each giving increasingly less subtle clues as to where they believe they are. Once three minutes is up, the players line up against the back wall. One player is called forward, and their teammates guess in unison where they think that player was. This repeats for all players.

**Variations on this Game**

- May be played with the referee getting time periods instead of locations. (Called *Mystery When*)

- May be played with the referee getting people or characters instead of locations. (Called *Mystery Who* or *Dysfunction Junction*)

# NIGHT AT THE BALLET

*"One player will watch a series of ballets, and have to guess what each one is about."*

One player is sent out of the room to be the guesser, and the referee will get a list of three historical events, movies, books, etc. The guesser is called back in and a timer is set for one minute.

The players will do a one minute ballet based on the first suggestion, after which the guesser will have to guess what it was about. Right or wrong, they move on to the second suggestion, then again for the third.

**Variations on this Game**

- May be played with the referee getting only historical events. (Called *Historical Ballet*)

- May be played with the referee getting only movies. (Called *Cinematic Ballet*)

- May be played with the referee getting only one suggestion, and breaking it into three acts. The guesser guesses the whole theme, and right or wrong the referee tells them the suggestion before having the guesser guess what each act was about.

- May be played head-to-head, with the guessers writing down their guesses.

# STICKER-DOODLES

*"The players will do a scene; the only problem is they don't know who they are."*

The referee sends the whole team out of the room, and gets a suggestion of an endowment for each player. These endowments can be characters, people, animals, an illness, etc., which are written on sticky notes or computer address labels. The players are called back in, the endowment is stuck to their back or forehead, and a timer is set for three minutes.

The referee gets a suggestion for the game, and the players begin to play a scene, each giving increasingly less subtle clues as to who the other players are. Once a player believes they know what their endowment is, they will take it on themself. When time runs out, the will step forward one at a time and guess who they are.

# THE QUEST

*"One player is about to go on a quest to search for and return five items."*

One player is sent out of the room to be the guesser, and the referee gets a list of five items. The guesser is called back in, and a timer is set for three minutes.

The guesser will start a scene with one of their teammates who will need an item, and give increasingly subtle hints as to what they need. Once the guesser has figured it out, they leave to get it. Another player comes onto the field and establishes a scene in a location where that item can be found, and will be willing to give them the item the previous player wanted if they can get something for them, giving hints as to what they need. This continues until the guesser knows what all five items are. Once they do they will go and retrieve the final item and return them all in reverse order. Only items returned before time runs out will count.

**Variations on this Game**

• May be played with guesser being a shopkeeper, and their teammates coming into the store to get the items with endowments. The guesser does not need to return them in reverse order in this variation. (Called "Shopping Spree" or "The Shoppe")

# GAMES NOT MENTIONED IN THIS SECTION

# HEAD-TO-HEAD GAMES

In any given home match, the teams will play at least three Head- to-Head Games. Having a mix of the games here leads to a more balanced match. While the primary categories aren't as cut and dry as with Team Games, still look at the objective of the game, the stage picture, and how it is played when choosing the games.

If a Head-to-Head Game is a variation of a Team Game, variations on games previously mentioned can be found by name in the index, or by looking for the similar game in the Team Games section. For example: "Six Things" will be found as a variation to "Five Things."

The purpose of Head-to-Head Games isn't to win, but to play the game well and in an entertaining fashion for the audience, with the players from both teams helping each other out.

Special Note: Most of the games found in the Team Games section can be played Head-to-Head, those which are most likely to be played as such are labeled as such in the variations, but you can try any game as a Head-to-Head, simply adapt them to fit your needs.

This section is broken down into five categories of games

- Scenic - These are games where the primary objective is a scenic based.

- Musical - These are games where the primary objective is to utilize music or dance. While these games can be easily put in other categories as well, as they all share the music aspect, they are here.

- Catch All - These are games where the primary objective is just in a world of its own, or they are too difficult to put into just one of the other categories. For simplicity's sake, they are just gathered here.

- Guessing - These are games where the primary objective is to showcase guessing and clue giving. These games can be played in the Go Ahead/Catch Up round, but due to their Head-to-Head nature, they are found here.

- Last Chance - These are games where the objective is to showcase the quick wittedness of players, utilizing puns, one liners, and other forms of step out jokes.

# SCENIC HEAD-TO-HEAD GAMES

Scenic head-to-head games are games in which the primary focus is storytelling or scene work. Generally, the games listed here are played by both teams during the Ref's Option/Head-to-Head round.

# 15 SECONDS EARLIER

*"One team will do a fifteen second scene, then the other team will show us what happened fifteen seconds leading up to that."*

The referee will get a suggestion for the game and determine which team will start. The first team will perform the last fifteen seconds of a scene, then the referee will switch teams. The second team will show fifteen seconds prior to the first scene, continuing to replay the original fifteen second scene as well, essentially making a thirty second scene. This continues back and forth with each team adding another fifteen seconds to the front of the scene

**Variations on this Game:**

- Ending by playing all of the parts in order.

# 55 WORDS

*"The teams will perform a scene; however, it must be exactly 55 words."*

The referee gets the suggestion for the game, and one player from each team will begin a scene. Throughout the scene the first line may only consist of one word, the second of only two, the third only of three, and so on until the tenth line consists of ten, for a title of 55 words. If any player makes a mistake, they are thrown out and a teammate will come in and start a new scene. If the two players make to 55 words, they both rotate out. This process continues for the rest of the game.

# BATTLESCENE GALACTICA

*"Both teams will do a scene using the same suggestion then you will decide which one you liked more."*

The referee will send one team out of the room, and get a suggestion for the game. The team in the room will perform their scene, then the other team returns is told the suggestion and perform a scene. Afterwards the audience votes for which scene they preferred.

# CONTINUATION

*"One team will start a scene, and at any point I may switch to the other team who will pick up exactly where the scene left off."*

The referee chooses which team will start the scene and gets a suggestion for the game. The team begins performing the scene, but at any point the referee will switch teams, who will have to pick up exactly where the other scene left off. This process continues for the rest of the game.

# DANCE PARTY

*"Both teams will dance, and I will call out specific players to do scenes based on their body positions."*

They referee calls both teams onto the field and the announcer will play music, to which all the players dance. Whenever the referee wishes, they will call "Freeze!" and the players will do so. The referee then picks certain players to do a quick scene based on their body positions. When the scene is done, the referee will declare "Everybody Dance!" and the process continues for the rest of the game.

**Alternate Names:** *Dance Freeze*

**Variations on this Game**

- May be played with one or more volunteer players. Your ref should not call on the volunteer players in the first scene or two, so they can get the idea of what's happening.

# DICK VAN DYKE

*"The players will show off their vocal prowess in a battle of accents."*

The referee gets the suggestion for the game, and a suggestion of an accent, dialect, or voice. One player from each team attempt to do a scene speaking with the suggested vocal endowment, but if the falter or fail to do a passable version, the referee will rotate them out and another player from their team will come in and try to do the endowed voice, picking up where the scene left off. The referee will switch the voice throughout the game.

# DON'T MAKE ME HECKLE

*"The teams will attempt to make each other break character in the scene by heckling them."*

The referee chooses which team will start the scene and gets a suggestion for the game. The team begins performing the scene, while the other team heckles them. If at any point one player in the scene laughs or breaks character, the other team rotates in and continues where the scene left off. The first team now gets to heckle them, trying to get them to break. This process continues for the rest of the game.

# ECHO

*"The lines of dialogue from our players will echo at the start of a scene from the other team."*

The referee gets a suggestion for the game and determines which team will start. The first team will begin a scene about the suggestion, and whenever the second team wishes they will clap their hands and say "Switch!" At this point the second team begins a scene beginning with the last line of dialogue from the previous scene exactly. This continues back and forth until the end of the game.

**Variations on this Game**

- May be played with the referee switching between the two teams as opposed to the players.

# FOREIGN TELEVISION

*"A lot of television shows are remakes of foreign shows, and the players will perform a few for you along with their English language versions."*

The referee chooses which team will start the scene and gets a suggestion for the name and genre of a made up foreign television show. The first team begins performing the scene in gibberish, and once they are done, the second team will perform it in English. The referee will then get a new suggestion of a title and genre, and the second team performs the gibberish scene followed by the first team performing the English language version.

# GOOGLE TRANSLATE

*"Two players will perform a scene, and then it will be sent through a gibberish translation."*

The teams separate into three pairs, the referee sends one pair out of the room, and gets a suggestion. The first pair of players will perform a two-person scene based on the suggestion, and are watched by the second pair in the audience. After the scene is done, the referee will call the third pair back in, who will watch the second pair perform the first scene in gibberish. After the gibberish scene is done, the third pair will perform it in English.

**Alternate Names:** *BabbleFish; Telephone*

**Variations on this Game**

- May be played with two pairs leaving the room, after the first scene and instead of a gibberish scene, a volunteer player describes the scene to the second pair in 10 seconds. The other volunteer watches the second scene and describes it to the third set of players using 10 word or less. This is usually called *Telephone*.

# GRAND THEFT AUTO

*"The players of one team will be going on a road trip, but the other team will come in and steal their car."*

The referee chooses what team will start the game, and get then gets a suggestion of two letters. The first team starts to act as though they are in a car on a road trip, while the second team begins to sneak up on the car. The player in the driver's seat notices them and declares "Oh no! It's ___!" giving them an endowment of two words, one word beginning with each initial from the suggestion, and abandon the car and exit the field. The second team takes on the endowment and begins to drive the car, while the first team sneaks up on them. The process continues for the rest of the game, and the referee may change the initials whenever they wish.

**Alternate Names:** Fire Drill

# I CAN DO BETTER

*"The players will perform a scene, but if another player thinks they can do better, they will challenge them."*

The referee chooses which team will start the scene and gets a suggestion for the game. The team begins performing the scene, and at any point in time a player from the other team can challenge them by declaring "I can do better!" The referee will ask the player what they can do better, and if the referee wants to see it the player will then tap out a player and attempt to do the proposed action better. If the referee deems it better, the scene continues with that player in it now. If the referee disagrees, the tapped-out player returns to the scene. This process continues for the rest of the game.

**Alternate Names:** Anything You Can Do

# I GIVE UP

*"Both teams will do a scene while I layer on challenges, the first team to mess up or give up loses."*

The referee gets the suggestion for the game, and one player from each team will begin a scene. Throughout the game, the referee will layer challenges on the teams, which if a team doesn't do or if a player says, "I Give Up!" they game is over and their team loses. These challenges can be anything the referee wishes from physical tasks the must do, endowments, genres, etc.

# LAUGH OUT

*"The teams will perform a dramatic scene, and if the audience laughs at something a player does or says that player will rotate out."*

The referee gets the suggestion for the game, and one player from each team will begin a scene. Throughout the scene if any player makes the audience laugh, they will be thrown out, and a teammate will come in and say the same line. This process continues for the rest of the game.

# MEANWHILE, ELSEWHERE

*"One team will start a scene, and if something inspires the other team they will say 'Meanwhile at...' and we will go to that scene."*

The referee chooses which team will start the scene and gets a suggestion for the game. The team begins performing the scene, and at any point in time a player from the other team may be inspired by something said and will say "Meanwhile at ___!" telling us the location of the next scene. The players on the field quickly exit, and the new scene begins in the location given, and loosely tied to the previous scene. This process continues for the rest of the game.

# MIRROR, MIRROR

*"The teams will move as mirrored images of each other, and I can switch back and forth between the two scenes."*

The referee chooses which team will start the scene and gets a suggestion of a location for each team. The first team begins performing the scene on one half of the field, while the second team mirrors their movements on the other half. When the referee wishes they will switch to the second team who will justify their positions in their location while performing a scene, while the first team now mirrors them. The referee switches back and forth between the two scenes, and the process continues for the rest of the game.

# PEN PALS

*"One player from each team will write a letter to a player from the other team and the players will act them out."*

The referee gets the suggestion of a relationship between two people and a time period, and decides which team will go first. The first team will send up on player who will take on one half of the relationship, and begin writing a letter to the other half of the relationship utilizing the styles of the era given, with their teammates acting out the letter, in a similar manner to the game "Dime Store Novel." The second team then does the same thing.

# QUESTIONS ONLY

*"The teams will battle head-to-head in a scene where they can only speak in questions. If a player messes up, their team will rotate."*

The referee gets the suggestion for the game, and one player from each team will begin a scene. The two players may only speak in questions, if a player fails to do so that player is rotated out for another player from their team to continue the scene.

**Variations on this Game**

• May be played with each line starting with the next letter of the alphabet instead of speaking only in questions. (Called "The Alphabet Game")

# SCOOP IT

*"One team will start a scene, and if something inspires the other team they will scoop that idea, and we will see a scene based on the idea."*

The referee chooses which team will start the scene and gets a suggestion for the game. The team begins performing the scene, and at any point in time a player from the other team may be inspired by something and will say "Scoop It!" and tell the referee what they want to scoop from the scene. The team on the field quickly exits, and the other team will do a scene based on what they scooped. This process continues for the rest of the game.

# STORY

*"I will conduct a story by pointing at players, who must pick up wherever the last player I was pointing to left off."*

The players line up at the front of the stage, and the referee gets a suggestion for the title of a story that has never been written. The referee will point at one player who will begin telling the story, and when the referee points at another player the previously pointed at player will stop speaking, and the new player will continue from where the last player left off. If ever a player fails to stop talk, doesn't pick up where the other player left off, repeats a word, or any other reason, the referee will throw them out. After a player is thrown own, the players begin a new chapter. This continues until only one player is left.

**Variations on this Game**

- May be played with the players dying dramatically whenever they are called out. (Called *Story, Story, Die*)

- May be played with the players reading from an instruction manual instead of telling a story. The referee will get the suggestions of different sections of an instruction manual in between when players are thrown out. (Called *Instruction Manual*). This is an excellent opener for Road Shows.

- May be played with the reciting of a Wikipedia article instead of a story, with the referee clicking on words throughout each round, as well as getting new suggestion for the base article whenever a player is called out. (Called *Wikipedia (Conducted)* or *Hyperlink*)

# SWITCH INTERVIEW

*"We are about to see a series of interviews on talk shows inspired by your suggestions."*

Two chairs are put onto the field, with one player from each team in them. The referee will get a suggestion for the talk show, and the player on the right becomes the interviewer, while the player on the left becomes the guest. After a quick interview scene, the referee will call switch, the interviewer leaves, the guest moves to the interviewer's chair to become the interviewer, and another player becomes the guest. The referee gets another suggestion and we see another interview scene. This process continues for the rest of the game.

# THREE ROOMS

*"We will see a series of scene, which I will switch through and the next scene will always start with the last line of the previous scene."*

The teams separate into pairs, and the referee gets a suggestion for each team. The first pair begins their scene, and at any point the referee will call "Switch!" and repeat the last line said. The first pair will exit the field, and the second pair will begin their scene with the last line of the previous scene. This process repeats for the third team, and continues for the rest of the game.

**Alternate Names:** The game's name will change dependent upon the number of pairs. For example, four pairs it becomes Four Rooms, five pairs it becomes Five Rooms, or for sixty-four pairs it becomes Sixty-Four Rooms.

# TWO CHAIRS

*"The players will do a series of scenes inspired by the locations of where two chairs might be."*

Two chairs are put onto the field, with one player from each team in them. The referee will get a suggestion of a location for where these two chairs are, and the players will do a short scene inspired by the chair position and the location given, until the referee calls "Move Those Chairs!" The players will then move the chairs to somewhere else on the field and exit, as two new players enter. The referee will get a new suggestion of a location, and the process continues for the rest of the game.

**Variations on this Game**

• May be played with one of the players assuming the roles of a reporter and an eye witness, starting each scene with the line "Breaking News! We're on location at \_\_\_\_" using the suggested location. (Called *On Location*)

# WORD AT A TIME EXPRESS

*"The players will be acting out and telling a story, one word at a time."*

The referee gets the suggestion for the game, and one player from each team will begin telling a story and acting it out one word at a time. If ever a player fails to only use one word, they are rotated out, a new player enters and a new scene is started with a new suggestion.

**Variations on this Game**

• May be played with both players acting out all characters together, still only speaking one word at time.

# WORLD WITHOUT A LETTER

*"The teams will battle head-to-head in a scene where they cannot use a specific letter anywhere in any of their words. If a player messes up, their team will rotate."*

The referee gets the suggestion for the game, a letter that is banned and one player from each team will begin a scene. The two players may only speak in lines which that letter doesn't exist in, if a player uses that letter, that player is rotated out for another player from their team to continue the scene. The referee may change the letter, or add a second letter whenever they wish.

# YAY BOO

*"The players will be telling a story one line at a time, with one player saying things to make you all say 'Yay!' and the other making you say 'Boo!'"*

One player from each team takes the field, and the referee gets a suggestion for the game. The first player will begin with a positive line of the story to make the audience say "Yay!" The second player will add to the story with a negative line to make the audience say "Boo!" This continues back and forth, until a player makes the audience respond in the opposite way as intended or is just confusing, when this happens the offending player rotates out, and another player from their team enters. The Yay and the Boo positions switch teams, and a new suggestion is gotten. This process continues for the rest of the game.

**Alternate Names:** *Boo Yay*

**Variations on this Game**

• May be played with the players telling positive and negative facts about the suggestion instead of telling a story.

# GAMES NOT MENTIONED IN THIS SECTION

# CATCH-ALL HEAD-TO-HEAD GAMES

Whereas the previous section category focused on head-to-head games which are based on stories and scenes, the games in this section focus more on a gimmick or hoop the players must play with. Generally, the games listed here are played by both teams during the Ref's Option/Head-to-Head round.

# AUDITION

*"The players will be auditioning for an upcoming production of a play with monologues from made up plays."*

The referee will get a list of adjectives and nouns, and begins to act as a casting director for a play. Alternating between teams, one player at a time will come up and introduce themselves and what play the will be auditioning from, and delivery a monologue from it. The title of the play is an adjective noun combination from the list, and the may also make up a genre that the play is. Once any suggestion is used, it is crossed of the list. This continues until all players have auditioned.

**Variations on this Game**

- May be played using them as the titles of songs the players will sing.

- May be played with the referee getting a list of celebrities with distinct voice and a list of well-known movies and television shows. The players the audition for the films and television show as the celebrities. (Called *Screen Test*)

# CASANOVA (18+)

*"The players will deliver pick-up lines one word at a time in an attempt to earn a volunteer player's favor."*

The referee asks for a volunteer player from the audience over the age of eighteen, and the teams line up on either side of the volunteer player. The referee gets a suggestion for a game and chooses a team to start. The first team delivers a pick-up line one word at a time based on the suggestion, and then the second team also delivers a pick-up line. The volunteer player chooses which they prefer, and the first player on each side rotates to the end of their line, and the whole process repeats with a new suggestion each time. This continues for the rest of the game.

**Warning:** Get consent from all players and your audience volunteer player before playing this game.

# RADIO

*"The players will each be a different station on a radio which I can tune to using my hand as a radio dial."*

The players line up at the front of the stage, and the referee gets a suggestion of a topic for each of their radio channels. The referee will use their hand as a radio tuner, going up and down the line of stations, with the players speaking whenever the referee is pointing at them. Players should try to pick up where the last player left off turning it into a part of their station.

**Variations on this Game**

- May be played in the dark with a flashlight as the pointer.

# SCATTERGORIES

*"The players will list items in a specific category, if they repeat or something not in the category they will have to put a hand up. Two hands up and they're out. The ref may hear an offer from a player and say, "Which is also..." and the player must come up with a new category on the spot. This becomes the ongoing category."*

The players line up at the front of the stage, and the referee gets a suggestion of a category. The referee will point at one player who will begin listing items in that category, and when the referee points at another player they continue to list things in the category. If ever a player fails to list something in the category, repeats an item previously listed, or any other reason, the referee will instruct them to put a hand up. The referee will then get a new category, and repeat the process. Once a player has two hands up, they are out. This continues until only one player is left.

**Alternate Names:** *Dirty Hand Randy; Left Hand Larry*

# SWIPE RIGHT

*"A volunteer player will be introduced to the Tinder profiles of a slew of characters, and will choose to swipe left or right. If they swipe left the character goes away, if they swipe right the go on a date."*

The referee asks for a volunteer player from the audience, and the teams line up off the field in an alternating fashion. One at a time they will step forward and introduce themself in character as if reading their Tinder profiles. If the volunteer player dislikes the profile they will swipe left, and if they like it they will swipe right and go on a date with that character. During the date, the volunteer player or referee may still swipe left, and players start introducing characters again. The process continues for the rest of the game.

**Alternate Names:** *Tinder Swipe*

# TOWN HALL / TOWN MEETING

*"This town is in turmoil and the only way to fix it is to hold a town hall meeting then vote."*

The players situate themselves in the audience, and the referee gets a suggestion of something the town is in turmoil over. One team is pro suggestion and the other is against it. The referee will act as the facilitator of the town hall meeting, calling first on a member of pro-suggestion team, who will in character introduce themself and state their case. Then the referee calls on a player who is against the suggestion, who will also introduce themself and state their case. This continues until all players have spoken. During the game, players are encouraged to also endow volunteer players to be members of their coalition.

**Variations on this Game**

- May be played with the captains of the teams serving as the facilitators.

- May be played with a suggestion of a common argument, such as pancakes or waffles, and each side taking a stand.

# TRY THAT ON FOR SIZE

*"The players will go back and forth doing the same motion, giving it different meaning each time."*

One player from each team will take the field, the referee will choose which team will go first, and then get the suggestion of an active activity. The first player starts doing the activity, and the second player mimics the movement as closely as possible. They then go back and forth giving the movement a different justification, followed by saying "Try that on for size!" If either player repeats a justification, changes the motion, doesn't make sense, or for any other reason, the referee will call on them to rotate out. A new player will take their place, and the referee will get a suggestion of a new active activity and the process continues as such until the end of the game.

**Alternate Names:** *Top That!*

**Variations on this Game**

- May be played saying *Top That* instead of "Try That on for Size" if playing in the UK.

- May be played with multiple players on each side moving and speaking in unison.

# TWO MINUTE EXPERT

*"The players are a panel of experts who will challenge each other's statements and try to be the last player standing."*

Both teams will line up on the back wall, the referee will get an area of expertise, pick a player to start speaking on the subject, and start a timer for two minutes. The selected player begins to speak on the topic, and throughout the game the players from the other team can challenge what was said, with a brief reasoning for the challenge. Time stops during the challenges. If the referee accepts the challenge, the player will take the place of the speaker. If the referee doesn't, the original speaker continues. This continues until the end of the time, and the last player in speaking wins for their team.

**Alternate Names:** *Challenge; Wikipedia; 9 out of 10; Expert Challenge; Last Second Expert; 90 Second Expert*

**Variations on this Game**

- May be played where the teams each debate in favor of a different suggestion, and determining which is best.

- May be played where the challenges may be "hyperlinks" to associated topics.

- May be played where the teams may challenge even their own players.

- May be played where the challenges become more and more ridiculous.

- Some cities play this game without ever stopping the timer.

# WHAT ARE YOU DOING?

*"The players will go back and forth asking each other what they are doing, and then will have to tell them anything other than what they are actually doing, which the player must start doing...you know what? You'll figure it out."*

One player from each team will take the field and the referee will determine who will initiate. The initiator will start miming an activity, the other player will ask "What are you doing?" The initiator will immediately stop and say anything other than what they were miming, and the second player starts doing whatever was said. The initiator follows suit and asks what the other player is doing, and the other player stops and says anything but what they are doing. The initiator will begin doing this activity. The game continues in this fashion until a player is called out for hesitating, actually saying what they were doing, or for any other reason the referee wishes to call them out. A new player rotates in for the player called out, and becomes the initiator. As the game progress the referee may layer on obstacles such as all actions have to be related to a given theme, start with initials, rhyme, or whatever they wish.

# GAMES NOT MENTIONED IN THIS SECTION

# MUSICAL HEAD-TO-HEAD GAMES

Musical head-to-head games are head-to-head games that involve musicality in one way or another, be it through song, dance, rapping, or all of the above. Whereas these games may fall into either of the two previous categories, as these focus on musical aspects, they are found in this section. Generally, the games listed here are played by both teams during the Ref's Option/Head-to- Head round.

# BEASTIE RAP / RUN DMC

*"The players will form rap posses who will complete each other's rhyme."*

Both teams take the field, standing on opposite sides in a formation of one player in the front and the others behind them, the referee gets a suggestion of a one syllable name, chooses a team to start, and the announcer plays a rap beat. The person in the front of the first team will set up a line that will end with the name given, and the players behind them say the name in unison. The person in the front of the second team will set up a line ending in a rhyme to the name, that the players behind must say in unison, a la the Beastie Boys style of rapping. This continues back and forth until a player hesitates, the players behind don't speak in unison, or for any other reason the referee deems unworthy. When this happens, the referee will rotate the team that failed, so a new front person takes the lead, gets a new name, and the game begins again. This process continues until the end of the game.

**Variations on this Game**

• May be played with the team also adding in a four-beat repetitive dance between each team's rhymes, similar to the dances seen in the game *What You Got?*

# CELEBRITY JAM

*"We have assembled a group of music superstars here to raise awareness for a made-up cause."*

All of the players take the field, and the referee will get a suggestion for made up cause. The players take on the characteristics and style of superstar musicians, and begin to sing a song about the cause, à la "We Are The World." The players will find their own ending.

**Alternate Names:** *Blank Aid*

# COMPILATION ALBUM

*"The players will debut songs from a new themed compilation album."*

The referee gets a suggestion for the game, and one player from each time will step onto the field and take on the personas of infomercial pitchmen. They will banter between themselves while introducing the style and name of songs on a new compilation album based on the suggestion. Once they have pitched a song, the remaining players will perform that song. This continues until four songs have been pitched and performed.

# DA DOO RON RON

*"Using your one syllable names and nicknames our players will perform a song for you in the style of the 1963 Crystals classic, Da Doo Ron Ron."*

The teams line up at the front of the field, alternating the players between the teams, and the referee gets the suggestion of a one syllable name or nickname. Using the rhyme scheme of the song "Da Doo Ron Ron," the players will make up a song. The first player will sing how they met the suggested name, followed by everyone singing "Da Doo Ron Ron Ron, Da Doo Ron Ron." The second player will sing a line that rhymes with the name, followed by all the players singing "Da Doo Ron Ron Ron, Da Doo Ron Ron" again. All the players now sing "Da-da-da-dum, yeah" then the third player makes a rhyme. Again, all the players sing "Da-da-da-dum, yeah" and the third player will make a second rhyme. Finally, all the players sing "Da-da-da-dum, yeah" and the third player makes a third rhyme. All players sing "Da Doo Ron Ron Ron, Da Doo Ron Ron" and the pattern continues for the remaining players in the same fashion for players one through three, wrapping around back to the beginning whenever it reaches the end of the line. The referee will encourage the audience to sing along. If ever a player hesitates, falls off rhythm, repeats a rhyme, or fails to rhyme with the name, the player is out. Whenever a player leaves the field, the referee will get a new suggested name, and the whole thing starts over. This continues until only one player is left, or all the players from one team are eliminated.

**Alternate Names:** *Da Doo Run Run*

**Variations on this Game**

- May be played in the style of rap, following the same rhyme structure, but replacing the choruses of "Da Doo Ron Ron Ron, Da Doo Ron Ron" with "Da Doo Rap Rap Rap, Da Doo Rap Rap," and "Da-da-da-dum, yeah" with "Say What?" (Called *Da Doo Rap Rap*)

- May be played with counting "5, 6, 7, 8!" as a lead in to the game and before the first singer of every group of three singers.

- May be played with getting a two-syllable name as the game progresses.

- May be played with the referee layering genres of music on the song.

- May be played getting faster as the game progresses.

# DANCE PARTY

*"Our players will be dancers on a hit dance show, teaching us all the new dances!"*

The referee will get a list of ten or so nouns, which the teams will each write down. The referee then takes on the persona of the host of a 1960s-style dance show and welcome a player onto the field. The player will pick a noun off the list to be the name of a dance, and jump on the field in as a character. The referee will interview the dancer, asking their name, where they're from, the name of the dance they will be doing, and how they came up with it. Once a dance is chosen, it cannot be performed again. After the interview, the announcer will play music and the dancer will do their dance for about 20-30 seconds. The referee will thank them, and call up a dancer from the other team, and repeat the process. Once all players have danced, the referee will call all the players onto the field to reprise their dances.

**Alternate Names:** *Hamster Scramble*

**Variations on this Game**

- May be played with players coming up in pairs.

# DUELING SOUNDTRACKS

*"One team will sing theme songs for never before seen shows, which the other team must act out a scene from."*

The referee decides which team will sing first, calls them onto the field, and get the suggestion for a made-up television show's title and genre. The first team will sing a short theme song for the show, endowing the other team with information about the show. The second team then acts out a quick scene from the show described in the theme song. After the scene, the referee will get a new set of suggestions, the second team sings the theme song, and the first team acts it out. This may be repeated multiple times, or just each team doing one song and one scene.

### Variations on this Game

- May be played with the referee conducting the theme song, pointing at the player they want to sing the next line.

# MUSICAL RUMBLE

*"Our players will be singers of your new favorite songs."*

The referee will get a list of ten or so nouns and a series of musical genres, which the teams will each write down. The referee then will welcome a player onto the field to be the first singer. The singer will introduce the song's name and genre. Once a noun and genre is chosen, it cannot be performed again. The singer then performs the song, the referee will thank them, and call up a singer from the other team, and the process repeats, alternating the teams between each song. Once all players have sung the game is done.

**Variations on this Game**

- May be played with players coming up in pairs.

- May be played with one player from each team each singing their own song based on the same suggestion, and the audience determining which was better. After the first round, two more sing about a new suggestion, and so on.

- May be played with the accompanist or announcer picking the player's song and genre for them.

# RHYME LINE

*"The players will rap, but if they hesitate, fail to rhyme, or fall of the rhythm, they are out."*

The players line up on the field in an alternating pattern, the referee will get a topic. The players will rap about the topic with the first player rapping the first half of a rhyming couplet and the second completing the couplet. The second player then raps the first half of a couplet for the third person to complete, and so on, and so on. Once the pattern reaches the end of the line it wraps back around to the first player in line. This continues until a player is eliminated for failing to rhyme or falling off the beat, then the referee gets a new topic and the game begins again. Once all but one player is left, they win for their team.

**Alternate Names:** *Elimination Rap; Rap Line*

**Variations on this Game**

- May be played with the player reciting love poetry instead of rapping. (Called *Love Poems*)

- May be played setting up the rhyme structure of a limerick. (Called *Limerick*)

# SING FOR YOUR SUPPER

*"The players will sing a song conducted by myself."*

The players form a line at the front of the field, and the referee gets a suggestion for them to sing about. The music begins and the referee begins to conduct the players, singing when the referee points at them individually or collectively. After a verse, the referee will have one player sing a three or four-word simple chorus, which all the other players join in on. This is sung after every verse, and at the very end.

**Variations on this Game**

- May be played with the referee interviewing a volunteer player instead of getting a suggestion.

- May be played unconducted, with the players sharing focus.

# WHAT YOU GOT?

*"The teams will engage in a dance battle, but if they fall off rhythm or off topic they will have to rotate."*

The teams form into dance posses, facing off on either side of the field. The referee will get a suggestion of a relationship between people, assign one side of the relationship to either dance posse, and determine who goes first. The first team's front player will say a line about their side of the relationship along with a movement to go along with it, then the rest of their team doing it with them two more times before saying, "What You Got?" The second team will respond in the same fashion, but with a line and action from their side of the relationship. This continues until a player falls off rhythm or off topic, at which point the referee will have that team rotate. Whenever a team rotates, the referee will get a new suggestion and the game starts again. This continues until the end of the game.

### Variations on this Game

- May be played with the referee getting suggestions of anything instead of just relationships.

# GAMES NOT MENTIONED IN THIS SECTION

# GUESSING HEAD-TO-HEAD GAMES

While most of the guessing games mentioned in the Team Game section may be played head-to-head through a variation and can be found there, there are a few guessing games which can only be played head-to-head. Those games can be found here. Generally, the games listed here are played by both teams during the Ref's Option/Head-to-Head round.

# GUESS THAT THING

*"The guessers will be put into an array of stories, and need to guess what stories they are in, while the teams bid down on how much time it would to take to get them to guess it."*

The referee sends one player from each team out of the room to be the guessers and gets a list of six-eight stories, video games, movies, plays, television shows, etc. The referee calls the guessers back in, and one teammate from each team will start bidding on how much time it will take to get across the suggestion to their guesser. When either team determines they can't go any lower they will turn to the audience and declare "Guess That Thing!" Using only pantomime and gibberish the team with the winning bid will put their guesser in the story trying to get it across in only the amount of time they bid. The guesser will guess, and if they get it wrong the other guesser may steal. The stories are done in the order that they were suggested. This continues until all stories have been guessed.

**Variations on this Game**

- May be played as a variation of the game *Six Things*.

- May be played the referee getting changes to the stories as well.

# I LOVE A PARADE

*"One player from each team will be the commentators on a parade, performed by their teammates."*

The referee sends one player from each team out of the room to be the guessers and gets a list of 8-12 stories, video games, movies, plays, television shows, etc. The referee calls the guessers back in, and they take on the personas of parade commentators. The rest of the players will work together to perform as floats that represent the stories suggested. The guessers go back and forth taking turns making guesses as to what they think the floats are while still commentating on the parade. Once a float is guessed, or it has crossed the field, the next float immediately follows. This continues until all stories have been shown as floats.

**Variations on this Game**

• May be played with the floats being replaced by zombies acting out the scenes. (Called *Zombie Parade*)

# PLAYGROUND INSULTS

*"One player from each team will be kids on a playground insulting each other, but like children are wont to do, they don't really know what insult they are trying to say."*

The referee sends one player from each team out of the room to be the guessers and gets the suggestion of an insult in the form of Adjective Verb-ing Noun, each word having three or more syllables. The guessers are called back in, and take on the personas of two kids arguing with and mildly insulting each other. The kids face each other with each having their back to the other team's clue givers. The referee will determine which team will go first, and their teammates will get across the first word by breaking it down into smaller syllable chunks and getting them across through pantomime. They first guesser will try to guess what the syllable is working their guesses into their insults. Every ten to twenty seconds, the referee will switch between the teams guessing. Once all of the syllables have been gotten across, the guesser will put them together to find the whole word. When the adjective word is guessed, the teams will move on to the second word, and then the third. The first guesser to call the other the full insult wins for their team.

**Variations on this Game**

- May be played as the players are debating the pros and cons of a Verb-ing Adjective Noun. (Called "Sideline Debate")

- May be played as the players are making an old-school dating service video looking for an Adjective Occupation who enjoys Verb-ing. (Called "Sideline Dating Service")

- May be played with the referee getting a list of multiword song titles, which the clue givers must get across while the guesser keeps singing. (Called "Sideline Karaoke")

- May be played and adapted to holidays and other occasions by changing the word gotten in the suggestion.

# GAMES NOT MENTIONED IN THIS SECTION

# LAST CHANCE GAMES

These games are the games generally played at the end of the match, hence the name last chance games. They encompass more traditional joke and pun style jokes, but there are a few exceptions.

# 185

*"The players will deliver jokes in the style of '185 blanks walk into a bar. The bartender says "What'll you have?", and the 185 blanks say punchline!'"*

Both teams line up along the back wall, and the referee will get a suggestion for the game. Whenever a player has a joke they will step forward and deliver it in the style of "185 (suggestions) walk into a bar. The bartender says, 'What'll you have?.' The 185 (suggestions) say (pun or punchline)." The referee may change the suggestion whenever they wish.

**Variations on the Game**

• May be played with the players replacing "Bar" and "Bartender" with "Restaurant" and "Manager" for teams that do not condone drinking, i.e. those under 18.

# BACK IN MY DAY

*"The players will tell us what it was like back in their day."*

Both teams line up along the back wall, and the referee will get a suggestion for the game. Whenever a player has a joke they will step forward as an old person and deliver it in the style of "Back in my day we didn't have (suggestion), (punchline)." The referee may change the suggestion whenever they wish.

# B MOVIE

*"The players will tell you about a bad movie they have recently seen."*

Both teams line up along the back wall, and the referee will get a suggestion for the game. Whenever a player has a joke they will step forward and start the delivery of a joke in the style of "I saw a movie about (suggestion) that was so (adjective)." The audience and other players will all respond with "How (adjective) was it?" The player then finishes the joke. The referee may change the suggestion whenever they wish.

**Variations on the Game**

- May be played with the players instead saying, "I caught a (suggestion) that was so (adjective)." The audience and other players will all respond with "How (adjective) was it?" The player then finishes the joke. (Called *Fisherman's Boast*)

# COMING SOON...

*"The players will tell us about the new movies coming out."*

Both teams line up along the back wall, and the referee will get a suggestion for the game. Whenever a player has a joke they will step forward as the voice of a movie trailer and deliver it in the style of "Coming soon to a theatre near you: (suggestion). (Punchline)." The punchline is in the form of the movie's tagline. The referee may change the suggestion whenever they wish.

# CRAIGSLIST

*"The players will buy or sell some interesting things on Craigslist, and tell us what happened."*

Both teams line up along the back wall, and the referee will get a suggestion for the game. Whenever a player has a joke they will step forward and start the delivery of a joke in the style of "I bought a (suggestion) on Craigslist. (Punchline)." With the punchline being based on what happened with the purchase. The referee may change the suggestion whenever they wish.

# DEAR DIARY,

*"The players will share the diary entries of famous people."*

Both teams line up along the back wall, and the referee will get a suggestion for a famous person or fictional character. Whenever a player has a joke they will step forward as and deliver it in the style of a diary entry for the suggested person. The referee may change the suggestion whenever they wish.

**Variations on this Game**

- May be played with the players leaving an outgoing or incoming voicemail message for the suggested person. (Called *Voicemail*)

- May be played with the players leaving tweets, as opposed to diary entries. (Called *Celebrity Twitter*)

- May be played with suggestions of anything, not just people.

# FANDAMONIUM

*"The volunteer player will do a repetitive motion, while the players justify the activity."*

Both teams line up along the back wall and the referee will ask for a volunteer player from the audience. The referee will then get a suggestion of an activity, which the volunteer player will do repeatedly. When the players have an idea, they will step forward and interact with the volunteer player, justifying different meaning each time. The referee may change the activity whenever they wish.

**Alternate Names:** *Fan Torture*

# GAME OF GROANS

*"The players will tell us about some of the lesser houses from Game of Thrones."*

Both teams line up along the back wall, the referee gets a suggestion for the game. Whenever a player has an idea they will step forward and declare "House (suggestion), (punchline)!" The punchline is a pun or joke slogan for the house, similar to those found for the houses in *Game of Thrones*. The referee may change the suggestion whenever they wish.

# GARTH

*"In the style of pop culture icon Garth Algar, our players will tell us what celebrities would be named if they were other things."*

Both teams line up along the back wall, and the referee will get a suggestion of a person for the game. Whenever a player has a joke they will step forward and start the delivery of a joke along the lines of "If (suggestion) was (something else), they'd be called (punchline)." The punchline is generally a mashup of the celebrity's name and whatever the other thing was, similar to the way Garth would in *Wayne's World*. The referee may change the suggestion whenever they wish.

# HEY, WAITER

*"A volunteer player will be letting a waiter know about the odd things they found in their soup."*

Both teams line up along the back wall, the referee will ask for a volunteer player from the audience, and get a suggestion for the game. Whenever a player has a joke they will step forward and hand a bowl of soup to the volunteer player, who will say "Hey waiter, there's a (suggestion) in my soup." To which the player will respond with a punchline based on the suggestion. The referee may change the suggestion whenever they wish.

**Variations on this Game**

- May be played with the volunteer player being a patient telling a doctor "Doctor, I have (suggestion). To which the player will respond with a punchline based on the suggestion. (Called *Bedside Manner*)

- May be played with the volunteer player being a speed dater saying, "I like (suggestion)." To which the player will respond with a punchline in the style of a pickup line. (Called *Speed Dating*)

- May be played with many adaptations to fit holidays and such, changing the phrase the volunteer says accordingly.

# I KISSED A BLANK

*"The players will tell us about a time they kissed something."*

Both teams line up along the back wall, and the referee will get a suggestion for the game. Whenever a player has a joke they will step forward and start the delivery of a joke in the style of "I kissed a (suggestion)." The audience and other players will all respond with "Really?" The player then finishes with a punchline explaining how the kiss was. The referee may change the suggestion whenever they wish.

# IT'S NOT YOU, IT'S ME

*"The players will deliver a breakup line based on your suggestion."*

Both teams line up along the back wall, and the referee will get a suggestion for the game. Whenever a player has a joke they will step forward and deliver it in the style of "It's not you, it's me. (Punchline)." The punchline a reason for breaking up with someone based on the suggestion. The referee may change the suggestion whenever they wish.

# JERSEY DINER

"The players will tell you why you don't want to order that."

Both teams line up along the back wall, and the referee will get a suggestion for the game. Whenever a player has a joke, they will step forward and deliver a joke in the style of "Oh, you don't want to order (suggestion). It's (punchline)" The referee may change the suggestion whenever they wish.

**Alternative names:** *Truckstop Diner; Roadside Diner*

# JIMMY THE PIGEON

*"The players will tell us about Jimmy the Suggestion."*

Both teams line up along the back wall, and the referee will get two suggestions for the game. Whenever a player has a joke they will step forward and start the delivery of a joke in the style of "Did you hear about Jimmy the (suggestion)." The audience and other players will all respond with "No!" The player then finishes with a telling us a punchline about Jimmy. The referee may change the suggestion whenever they wish.

**Variations on this Game**

- Players may call other players out: "Hey, [player], did you hear about Jimmy the _____? The other player says, "No!" and the first player delivers the punchline. The second player may immediately add their own punchline.

# LAST ACTION JOKE

*"The players will deliver a joke in the style of Arnold Schwarzenegger's trademarked wit."*

Both teams line up along the back wall, and the referee will get a suggestion of an object for the game. Whenever a player has a joke they will step forward and pantomime attacking a bad guy with the suggestion, and then deliver a punchline in the style of Arnold Schwarzenegger's older films. The referee may change the suggestions whenever they wish.

**Variations on this Game**

• May be played with the players taking on the persona of David Caruso of CSI: Miami, and finding a person attacked rather than doing the attacking. The players deliver the punchline while removing sunglasses. (Called *CSz: Miami*)

# LET ME TELL YOU SOMETHING, BROTHER

"The players will deliver a joke in the style of a professional wrestler."

Both teams line up along the back wall, and the referee will get a suggestion for the game. Whenever a player has a joke, they will step forward and deliver a pun based insult in the style of professional wrestlers like Hulk Hogan or the Rock. The referee may change the suggestions whenever they wish.

# LETTERS FROM CAMP

*"The players will be kids writing home from summer camps themed around your suggestion."*

Both teams line up along the back wall, and the referee will get a suggestion of anything at all. Whenever a player has a joke they will step forward and delivery it as if a child writing home from a camp themed around the suggestion, with the jokes being puns or references surrounding camp life.

# OBJECT FREEZE

*"The players will be given a random object, which they will have to use in anyway but normal."*

At half time, the referee asks audience to go to their cars and get unusual objects. When it comes time to play the game, before each object is brought out onto the field during the game, both teams line up along the back wall with their backs turned to the audience. The referee places a random object on the field. Players turn around and step forward when they have an idea and use the object in any way other than what the object actually is. The referee may have they players turn their backs and change the item whenever they wish.

**Alternate Names:** *Object Tag; Props*

# PHONE HOME

*"The players will be aliens phoning home to tell them about things found on Earth."*

Both teams line up along the back wall, and the referee will get a suggestion for the game. Whenever a player has a joke they will step forward and as an alien phoning home to tell them about the suggestion. The jokes can be pun-based, misinformation, or anything the player wishes. The referee may change the suggestion whenever they wish.

# SMACKDOWN

*"The players will tell us about fights and who won."*

Both teams line up along the back wall, and the referee will get two suggestions for the game. Whenever a player has a joke they will step forward and start the delivery of a joke in the style of "A (suggestion one) fought a (suggestion two)." The audience and other players will all respond with "Who won?" The player then finishes with a telling us who won and a punchline telling us why. The referee may change the suggestions whenever they wish.

# TSA

*"The players will be TSA agents and find some strange things in people's luggage."*

Both teams line up along the back wall, and the referee will get a suggestion for the game. Whenever a player has a joke they will step forward and as a TSA agent who found the suggestion in a bag, delivering a punchline based on the suggestion. The referee may change the suggestion whenever they wish.

# WHATCHA GET?

*"The players will tell us about things they have crossed together."*

Both teams line up along the back wall, and the referee will get a suggestion for the game. Whenever a player has a joke they will step forward and start the delivery of a joke in the style of "I crossed a (suggestion) with (something else)." The audience and other players will all respond with "Whatcha get?" The player then finishes with a punchline telling us what they got. The referee may change the suggestion whenever they wish.

**Variations on this Game**

- May be played with the referee getting both things that are crossed.

# WHEN I GROW UP

*"The players will tell us what they want to be when they grow up."*

Both teams line up along the back wall, and the referee will get a suggestion for the game. Whenever a player has a joke they will step forward as a young child and deliver it in the style of "When I grow up I want to be (suggestion), (punchline)." The referee may change the suggestion whenever they wish.

# WORLD'S WORST

*"The players will show us the world's worst versions of different things."*

Both teams line up along the back wall, and the referee will get a suggestion for the game. Whenever a player has a joke they will step forward and portray the world's worst version of the suggestion. The referee can get suggestions of occupations, a product or location to give ad slogans for, or an event where things are said. The referee may change the suggestion whenever they wish.

**Variations on this Game**

- May be played with the referee getting only locations and events, with the players telling us things you would never hear there. (Called *Things You Never Hear*)

- May be played with the referee getting only suggestions of products and locations. (Called *Slogans*)

- May be played with the referee getting only suggestions of locations. (Called *Punnsylvania*)

# GAMES NOT MENTIONED IN THIS SECTION

# STREAMING GAMES

Although many of the other 300+ games in this book can be played in an online format, perhaps with some modifications, this section focuses on games that can only be played online and taking advantage of that technology. Most of these games were developed using the Zoom platform and terminology will reflect that. If you are using a different platform like OBS, you will want to explore those offerings to see if the games can be adapted.

These games aren't separated by team or head-to-head. Instead, the classifications will be listed under the game name.

# ANTIQUES ROADSHOW
## HEAD-TO-HEAD

"The players will show items from somewhere around them and link them to a suggestion we'll get from you, and they'll be evaluated by our antique experts"

The referee asks for a theme that all the collectables will be related to. One player from each team serves as the antiques experts. The rest of the players will take turns showing random items from their playspace to. The experts will ask questions to help further define the items ("Are there special markings?" or "What does it taste like?") The experts end each interaction by giving an estimated value for the item.

**Variations on this game:** May be played as a single team game with the ref playing the expert

# DIRECTOR'S COMMENTARY
## SINGLE TEAM

"The players will provide the commentary tracks from the DVD of a movie they don't know"

The referee asks for a variety of jobs on a movie set that aren't frequently featured (so no actors or directors) and a made-up movie title. A movie clip will begin playing and the players will discuss what's happening based on their assigned jobs and influenced by the movie title. Players have their cameras off for this game. Movie clips should be screened ahead of time to make sure there is no inappropriate content.

# DUB CLUB
## SINGLE TEAM

"The players will provide the voices for a movie they don't know"

The referee asks for a suggestion. A movie clip will begin playing silently and the players provide the voices for the scene, influenced by the suggestion. Players have their cameras off for this game. Movie clips should be screened ahead of time to make sure there is no inappropriate content and to make sure how many character voices will be needed.

# GRAMMA-PHONE
## HEAD-TO-HEAD

"The players all want to talk to Grandma on the phone. They will take turns but before they hand the phone over they will introduce the next person using initials we'll get from you"

The referee asks for sets of initials. One player begins talking to the grandmother on the phone. Once the next player turns their camera on, the first player introduces the next player with the suggested initials being the endowment for who will be taking over on the phone. Once they mime handing off the phone, the first player turns off their camera and the second player talks on the phone with grandma as that endowed character, until the third player turns on their camera and gets introduced. This rotates through the players and the referee can switch to another set of initials at any point.

# MISGUIDED MEDITATION
## SINGLE TEAM

"One of the players will guide a meditation, inspired by images drawn by the other players"

The referee asks for a topic for the meditation to be about. Using the whiteboard function, one player serves as a guide for a meditation while new age music is played for further relaxation. The other players on the team will be drawing images that the guide will have to describe and incorporate into what they're saying. If the guide says to take a deep breath, that's a good time to clear the white board and start with fresh images.

# NEAR, FAR, WHEREVER YOU ARE
## SINGLE TEAM

"The players will play out a scene but one player must be close to their camera, one must be far from their camera, and one must be off camera. No two players can be in the same situation"

The referee gets a suggestion for the scene. One player starts very close to their camera and another very far from their camera. The positions will change within the scene, much like Sit Stand Kneel. A third character in the scene has to be off camera.

# PASS THE MIC
## HEAD-TO-HEAD

"The players go back and forth giving lines rhyming single syllable names"

The referee asks for single syllable names. One player from each team starts. The first player starts similar to Da Doo Run Run with "I knew this guy, his name was ____" then the two players take turns laying rhyming lines with "Pass the Mic, Pass the Mic" in between. If a player repeats, falls off the rhythm, fails to rhyme, or any violation of the ref's choosing, they have to rotate out.

# PIF (PUBLIC INFORMATION FILM)
## SINGLE TEAM

"The players will provide the educational narration of a film"

The referee gets a topic for an educational film. A movie clip will begin playing and the players will provide the narration for the film. Players have their cameras off for this game. **Movie clips should be screened ahead of time to make sure there is no inappropriate content.**

**Alternate names:** PSA

# SORKIN
**SINGLE TEAM**

"The players will play out a scene, however at any point I can say 'Sorkin' and they'll have to do a walk and talk"

The referee gets a suggestion for the scene. All the players should be streaming from their phone or an unplugged laptop, because at any point the referee may identify a player to Sorkin, and that player must immediately pick up their camera and while continuing their dialogue walk to a different location until the referee instructs them to stop. The referee will rotate through the players and can even call all players to move at once.

# SPECIAL DELIVERY

"The players will be delivering items based on your suggestions."

Both teams line up along the back wall, and the referee will get a suggestion for the game. Whenever a player has a joke, they will step forward and start the delivery of a joke in the style of "Ding- dong. I've got your (suggestion)." The ref will respond with "Yes?" or some other appropriate acknowledgement. The player then finishes with a punchline related to the item. The referee may change the suggestion whenever they wish.

**Alternate name:** *Put It On The Porch*

# TELEPROMPTER MUSICAL
## SINGLE TEAM

"Players will sing a lovely song for you as their teammates type out the lyrics"

The referee asks a made-up song title. The white board function is started and two players will be typing song lyrics, leaving any typos in place, while one or two players sing what is being typed. The singers are the only ones with their cameras on.

**Variations of this game:**
- May be played with one player dancing and one player singing;

- The second typist could be from the other team, the announcer, or the chat wrangler;

- May be played without music, with the words being read by a newscaster. (Called *Teleprompter Newscast*)

# GAMES NOT MENTIONED IN THIS SECTION

# GAME LISTS

Here is a full games list of the 300+ games mentioned in this book. If it is not on these lists, check the index, as it could be listed under an alternate name.

If a game can be played as a Head-to-Head game, as well as a team game, it is noted with this symbol: **H**

If a game can be played with an audience volunteer, but isn't necessarily a volunteer player game, it is noted with this symbol: **V**

Games that have worked well on Zoom / Streaming are marked with this symbol: **Z**

Games that newer ComedySportz teams should learn early on are marked with this symbol: **N**

# TEAM GAMES LIST

## INTERRUPT GAMES

- Accent Roller Coaster Z
- Alexa Z
- Are You Thinking What I'm Thinking?
- Awkwarder
- Back To Whenever
- Bad Kitty
- Big Little Z
- Calvin Ball
- Center of Attention - V
- Changing Emotions Z
- Changing Emotions and Stuff
- Choose Your Own Adventure
- Conjunction Junction
- Copycat
- D&D in The Life
- Death Pendulum
- Deeper
- DVD Z
- Evil Twin
- Fabric of Time Z
- Forward in Verse
- Forward Reverse Z

- Foursquare - V Z
- Foursquare Dubbing
- Freeze Tag - H N
- Gibberish Switch
- Growing Shrinking Machine  N Z
- I Dream of Jeannie
- I Gotta Take This
- Identity Crisis
- Inner Monologue - H  Z
- Interrupting Zebra
- Jeanne's Nightmare
- New Choice  Z N
- New Rhyme
- Nitty Britty
- Old Time Comic
- Oscar Winning Moment  Z
- Parallel Universe
- Pileup
- Scantron
- Scene in Reverse
- Seuss Switch
- Shakespeare Switch
- Shrinking Growing Machine
- Soap Opera - H  Z
- Spin-Off - H
- Start Over - H
- Stunt Double

- Switch
- Synonym Roll
- Tag Team Monologue
- Teen Choice Awards

# REPLAY GAMES
- Basic Replay - H  Z N
- Big Fish - H
- Countdown  N
- Groundhog's Replay
- Highlander
- Multiplicity
- Multiverse
- Naive Replay
- Pileup Replay
- Replay at Bernie's
- Skewed
- Temporal Replay

# JUSTIFICATION GAMES
- Acromania
- Dime Store Novel  N
- Entrances And Exits - H
- Fortune Cookies
- Instant Soap Opera  Z N
- Interpreter - V  Z N
- Limit Line

- Memento
- Offstage Directions
- Oxygen Deprivation (18+)
- Pavlovian Response
- Pick A Play - V Z N
- Pick-up Lines N
- Revolving Doors
- Sit Stand Kneel Lie
- Stage Directions
- Stand By Scene - V
- Subtext - V
- Texts From Tonight - V
- Uncle Gibberish - V

# VOLUNTEER PLAYER GAMES

- Arms Expert
- Audience Sound Effects N
- Bedtime Story H
- Campfire Story H
- Coffee Break
- Columns
- Day In The Life H Z N
- Dinner At Joe's - H
- Double Speak
- Foreign Movie N
- Hesitation
- Laughterhouse 5
- Moving Bodies

- Newscaster - H Z
- Slide Show
- Slo-Mo  H N Z
- Talk Radio
- Teleprompter
- The Event  H
- What If?  H
- Word From Our Sponsor -V

# MUSICAL GAMES

- A Capella Jam - H
- Audience & Hammerstein  Z
- Blank! The Musical - H
- Blues Jam - H
- Four Crooners
- Gibberish Opera  H V
- Inner Songologue  H
- Ipso Facto Opera  H
- Kick It
- Lounge Lizards – H V Z
- Madrigal  N
- Musical Comedy  H Z
- Musical Genre  H
- My Songy  H
- No Time For Musicals
- Opera  H  Z

- Piano Torture
- Pick-up Line Musical
- Rap Madrigal
- Rap Switch
- Rock Opera  H
- Schoolhouse Mock Sham-Elton - H
- Sing It  N
- Slamlet
- [Source] Award Winning Moment
- That Gets A Bad Rap
- That Sounds Like A Song
- Three-Headed Broadway Star  V
- Tin Pan Alley  H
- Tony Winning Moment  Z

# CATCH-ALL

- AB Scene
- Acronym Panel  N
- Advice Panel  V  N
- Afterschool Special  H
- Alphabet Genre  H
- Barnyard Symphony  H
- Buzzfeed  H
- Career Fair
- Chameleon
- Critic - H

- Dr. Know-It-All - V N Z
- Dr. Share-A-Tongue V
- Dubbing H V
- Dumbbell Races Genre Piece H
- Emotional Rollercoaster
- Emotional Symphony H N
- Expert Panel V
- Factfinder H
- Fictional Eulogy - H
- Finishing School
- Flash Phrase H
- Game-O-Matic
- Good, Bad, Blank Advice
- Good, Bad, Worse Advice N Z
- If Blanks Ruled The World - H
- Marshmallow
- Mousetrap (18+)
- Mundane Zombie Attack - H
- My Movie - H
- New Fall Line Up - H
- Noir - H
- No See, No Hear, No Speak
- Oracle V N
- Remake - H
- Sears Family Portrait H
- Shakespeare H
- Spelling Bee N

- Spork River  H
- Studio Audience  H
- Superhero Eulogy  H
- Teen Drama  H
- Three-Way Dubbing
- Toots McGoots
- Yearbook  H

# GUESSING GAMES

- 1-2-3-4-5 Things  N Z
- Animatronic Jamboree  H V
- Blitz
- Chain Murder  V N
- Cinematic Ballet  H V
- Crystal Ball
- Dating Game
- Dysfunction Junction
- Five Things  N
- Historical Ballet - HV
- Hostage Negotiator
- Hot Bell  H V
- Interrogation
- Line Detector
- Lunch Break  V
- Movie Five Things
- Mystery When

- Mystery Where
- Mystery Who
- Pep Talk
- Night At The Ballet  H V
- Press Conference
- Shopping Spree  H Z
- Sticker-Doodles
- Sweet Sixteen
- The Quest
- Wedding Planner

# HEAD-TO-HEAD GAMES LIST

## SCENIC HEAD-TO-HEAD GAMES

- 15 Seconds Earlier
- 55 Words
- Babble Fish
- Battlescene Galactica
- Continuation
- Dance Party  V
- Dick Van Dyke
- Don't Make Me Heckle
- Echo
- Foreign Television
- Grand Theft Auto
- I Can Do Better

- I Give Up
- Instruction Manual   N Z
- Laugh Out
- Meanwhile, Elsewhere
- • Mirror, Mirror
- On Location
- Pen Pals
- Questions Only
- Scoop It

# CATCH-ALL HEAD-TO-HEAD GAMES

- Audition
- Casanova (18+)  V
- Dr. Debate  V
- Limerick
- Love Poems
- Radio
- Scattergories
- Screen Test
- Story Z N
- Switch Interview Z N
- Tag Team Tale
- The Alphabet Game
- Three Rooms Z N
- Tinder Swipe - V
- Town Hall Meeting - V  Z
- Try That On For Size  Z N

- Two Minute Expert Story
- Two Chairs N
- What Are You Doing? N Z
- Wikipedia (Challenge)
- Wikipedia (Conducted)
- Word At A Time Express
- World Without A Letter
- Yay Boo  N Z

# MUSICAL HEAD-TO-HEAD GAMES

- Beastie Rap
- Celebrity Jam
- Compilation Album
- Da Doo Rap Rap
- Da Doo Ron Ron
- Dance Party – V
- Dueling Soundtracks Z
- Musical Rumble
- Rap Line
- Sing For Your Supper
- What You Got? N

# GUESSING HEAD-TO-HEAD GAMES

- Bedside Manner - V
- Celebrity Twitter
- Coming Soon
- Craigslist

- Fandamonium - V
- Fisherman's Boast
- Four Things
- Game Of Groans
- Garth
- Guess That Thing
- Hey, Santa  V
- Hey, Waiter  V
- I Love A Parade  V
- Playground Insults
- Sideline Dating Service
- Sideline Debate
- Sideline Karaoke
- Six Things
- Zombie Parade  V

# LAST CHANCE GAMES

- 185 N Z
- B-Movie N Z
- Craigslist
- CSz Miami
- Dear Diary,
- I Kissed A Blank
- It's Not You, It's Me  Z
- Jimmy The Pigeon  Z
- Last Action Joke
- Letters From Camp  N Z
- Object Freeze  N

- Phone Home
- Punnsylvania
- Slogans
- Smackdown
- Speed Dating V
- Things You Never Hear
- TSA
- Voicemail
- When I Grow Up
- Whatcha Get?
- World's Worst

# STREAMING GAMES

- Antiques Roadshow
- Director's Commentary
- Dub Club
- Gramma Phone
- Misguided Meditation
- Near, Far, Wherever You Are
- Pass the Mic
- PIF – Public Information Film
- Put It On The Porch
- Sorkin
- Special Delivery
- Teleprompter Musical
- Teleprompter Newcast

# INDEX

1-2-3-4-5 Things · 153, 154
15 Seconds Earlier · 167
185 · 224
3 Rooms - 188
55 Words · 168
9 out of 10 · 202
90 Second Expert · 202

## A

A Capella Jam · 108
AB Scene · 118
ABC Scene · 118
Accent Roller Coaster · 22
Acromania · 64
Acronym Panel · 119
Action Figures · 92
Actor's Nightmare · 73
Advice Panel · 120
Afterschool Special · 131
Alexa · 18
Alphabet Genre · 121
Animatronic Jamboree · 148
Antiques Roadshow · 250
Anything You Can Do · 178
Are You Thinking What I'm Thinking · 19
Arms · 82
Arms Expert · 82
Audience & Hammerstein · 102
Audience Sing Along · 102
Audience Sound Effects · 83
Audition · 195

Aunt Gibberish · 79
Awkwarder · 25

## B

B Movie · 226
Babble Fish · 176
Back In My Day · 225
Back To Whenever · 20
Bad Kitty · 35
Ballet · 160
Bananas · 133
Barnyard Symphony · 127
Basic Replay · 50
Battlescene Galactica · 169
Beastie Rap / Run DMC · 206
Bedside Manner · 233
Bedtime Story · 84
Big Fish · 51
Big Little · 21
Blank Aid · 207
Blank! The Musical · 103
Blind Dubbing · 125
Blind Freeze Tag · 28
Blind Line · 74
Blind Line Musical · 74
Blind Sound Effects · 83
Blitz · 149
Blues Jam · 108
Boo Yay · 192
Buzzfeed · 122

## C

Calvin Ball · 30
Campfire Story · 84
Career Fair · 132
Casanova · 196

Celebrity Jam · 207
Celebrity Twitter · 229
Center Of Attention · 27
Chain Murder · 150
Challenge · 202
Chameleon · 126
Changing Emotions · 22
Changing Emotions and Stuff · 22
Changing Genres · 22
Changing Styles · 22
Changing Voices · 22
Choose Your Own Adventure · 40
Chubby Bunny · 133
Cinematic Ballet · 160
Coffee Break · 85
Columns · 86
Coming Soon... · 227
Compilation Album · 208
Conjunction Junction · 23
Continuation · 170
Copycat · 28
Countdown · 52
Craigslist · 228
Crime Story · 157
Critic · 123
Crystal Ball · 151
CSz Miami · 238

# D

D&D In The Life · 24
Da Doo Rap Rap · 210
Da Doo Ron Ron · 209
Da Doo Run Run · 209
Dance Freeze · 171
Dance Party · 171
Dating Game · 152

Day In The Life · 87
Day in the Life: Shakespeare · 87
Dear Diary, · 229
Death Pendulum · 39
Deeper · 25
Dick Van Dyke · 172
Dime Store Novel · 65
Dinner At Joe's · 88
Director's Commentary · 251
Dirty Hand Randy · 198
Don't Make Me Heckle · 173
Double Dating Game · 152
Double Speak · 89
Dr. Debate · 124
Dr. Know-It-All · 124
Dr. Share-A-Tongue · 124
Dubbing · 125
Dub Club · 252
Dueling Soundtracks · 212
Duets · 27
DVD · 26
Dysfunction Junction · 159

# E

Echo · 174
Elimination Rap · 214
Eliminator Replay · 53
Emotional Party · 126
Emotional Rollercoaster · 126
Emotional Symphony · 127
Entrances And Exits · 75
Eulogy · 143
Everyday Olympics · 95
Evil Twin · 44
Expert Challenge · 202
Expert Panel · 120

Extreme Five Things · 153
Extreme Naive Replay · 58

## F

Fabric of Time · 22
Factfinder · 136
Family Dinner · 88
Fan Torture · 230
Fandamonium · 230
Fictional Eulogy · 143
Finishing School · 128
Fire Drill · 177
Fisherman's Boast · 226
Five Rooms · 188
Five Things · 153
Flash Phrase · 129
Flashback · 20
Foreign Movie · 90
Foreign Television · 175
Fortune Cookies · 74
Forward In Verse · 26
Forward Reverse · 26
Four Crooners · 27
Four Rooms · 188
Four Things · 154
Foursquare · 27
Foursquare Dubbing · 27
Foursquare Sound Effects · 27
Freeze · 28
Freeze Tag · 28

## G

Game Of Groans · 231
Game-O-Matic · 130
Garth · 232
Genre Piece · 131

Genre Replay · 50
Gibberish Opera · 104
Gibberish Switch · 45
Good, Bad, ___ Advice · 120
Good, Bad, Worse Advice · 120
Google Translate · 176
Gramma Phone · 253
Grand Theft Auto · 177
Groundhog's Replay · 54, 55
Growing Shrinking · 29
Growing Shrinking Machine · 29
Guess That Thing · 219

## H

Half-Life · 52
Hamster Scramble · 211
Hats · 32
Heavy Rotation · 32
Helping Hands · 82
Hesitation · 86
Hey Morty · 37
Hey Siri · 18
Hey, Waiter · 233
Highlander · 53
Historical Ballet · 160
Hostage Negotiator · 155
Hot Bell · 156
Hot Mustard · 133
Human Puppets · 92
Human Statues · 92
Hyperlink · 186

## I

I Can Do Better · 178
I Dream Of Jeannie · 30
I Give Up · 179

I Gotta Take This · 31
I Kissed A Blank · 234
I Love A Parade · 220
Identity Crisis · 32
If Blanks Ruled The World · 132
Inner Monologue · 33
Inner Songologue · 33
Instant Soap Opera · 67
Instruction Manual · 186
Interpreter · 66
Interrogation · 157
Interrupting Zebra · 34
Ipso Facto Opera · 105
It Could Happen · 132
It's Not You, It's Me · 235

## J

Jersey Diner · 236
Jimmy The Pigeon · 237

## K

Kick It · 112

## L

Last Action Joke · 238
Last Second Expert · 202
Laugh Out · 180
Laughterhouse 5 · 91
Left Hand Larry · 198
Let's Get Together · 88
Letters From Camp · 240
Lie Detector · 158
Limerick · 214
Limit Line · 68
Line Detector · 158

Lines from the Audience · 65
Lounge Lizards · 106
Love Poems · 214
Lunch Break · 150

# M

Madrigal · 107
Marshmallow · 133
Meanwhile, Elsewhere · 181
Mega Extreme Naive Replay · 58
Mega Growing Shrinking · 29
Mega Naive Replay · 58
Mega Replay · 50
Mega Ultra Naive Replay Memento · 69
Memento - 69
Mirror, Mirror · 182
Misguided Mediation · 254
Mousetrap · 134
Movie Five Things · 154
Movie Review · 123
Moving Bodies · 92
MTV Movie Awards · 38
Multiplicity · 56
Multiverse · 57
Mundane Olympics · 95
Mundane Zombie Attack · 135
Musical Comedy · 108
Musical Genre · 108
Musical Rumble · 213
My Movie · 136
My Songy · 136
Mystery When · 159
Mystery Where · 159
Mystery Who · 159

## N

Naive Replay · 58
Near, Far, Wherever You Are · 255
Negotiator · 155
New Choice · 35
New Fall Line Up · 136
New Rhyme · 35
Newscaster · 93
Night At The Ballet · 160
Nitty Britty · 36
No-Peek Freeze Tag · 28
No See, No Hear, No Speak · 137
No Time For Musicals · 112
Noir · 131
NPR · 96

## O

Object Freeze · 241
Object Tag · 241
Offstage Directions · 70
Old School Stand-Up · 37
Old Time Comic · 37
On Location · 189
Opera · 108
Oracle · 124
Oscar Winning Moment · 38
Our Town · 141
Oxygen Deprivation · 71

## P

Parallel Universe · 39
Pass The Mic · 256
Pavlovian Response · 72
Peeps · 133
Pen Pals · 183

Penny For Your Thoughts · 33
Pep Talk · 155
Phone Home · 242
Piano Torture · 109
Pick A Play · 73
Pick Up Lines · 74
Pick Up Line Musical – 74
PIF (Public Information Film) · 257
Pileup · 22
Pileup Replay · 50
Pillars · 86
Playground Insults · 221
Press Conference · 155
Pretty, Pretty Princess · 27
Props · 241
PSA · 257
Punnsylvania · 247
Put It On The Porch · 259

# Q

Questions Only · 184

# R

Radio · 197
Rap Line · 214
Rap Madrigal · 107
Rap Switch · 45
Reboot · 138
Remake · 138
Remote Dubbing · 125
Remote Sound Effects · 83
Replay · 50
Replay At Bernie's · 59
Replay at Bernie's Spinning Wheel of Death · 59
Replay-cement · 57
Revolving Doors · 75

Rock Opera · 108
Rube Goldberg · 72

## S

Scantron · 40
Scene In Reverse · 26
Scene on Book · 73
Schoolhouse Mock · 110
Scoop It · 185
Screen Test · 195
Sears Family Portrait · 139
Seuss Switch · 45
Shakespeare · 131
Shakespeare Switch · 45
Sham-ilton · 111
Shopping Spree · 162
Shrinking Growing · 29
Sideline Dating Service · 221
Sideline Debate · 221
Sideline Karaoke · 221
Sing For Your Supper · 215
Sing It · 112
Sit Stand Kneel Lie · 76
Six Things · 154
Skewed · 60
Slamlet · 45
Slide Show · 94
Slogans · 247
Slo-Mo · 95
Smackdown · 243
Soap Opera · 41
Sorkin · 258
Special Delivery · 259
Speed Dating · 233
Spelling Bee · 140
Spin-Off · 42

Spooky Bedtime Story · 84
Spoon River · 141
Spork River · 141
Stage Directions · 74
Stand By Scene · 77
Start Over · 43
Sticker-Doodles · 161
Story · 186
Story, Story, Die · 186
Studio Audience · 142
Stunt Double · 44
Subtext · 78
Subtitles · 90
Superhero Eulogy · 143
Sweet Sixteen · 155
Swipe Right · 199
Switch · 45
Switch Interview · 187
Symphony · 127
Synonym Roll · 46

## T

Tag Team Monologue · 47
Tag Team Musical · 47
Tag Team Tale · 47
Take My Pants · 143
Talk of the Town · 96
Talk Radio · 96
Teen Choice Awards · 38
Teen Drama · 131
Telephone · 176
Teleprompter · 86
Teleprompter Musical · 260
Teleprompter Newscast · 260
Temporal Replay · 61
Texts From Last Night · 78

Texts From Tonight · 78
That Gets a Bad Rap · 113
That Sounds Like A Song · 113
The Alphabet Game · 184
The Event · 97
The Fart Game · 145
The Quest - 162
The Shoppe · 162
Things You Never Hear · 247
Three Rooms · 188
Three-Headed Broadway Star · 114
Three-Way Dubbing · 125
Tin Pan Alley · 115
Tinder Swipe · 199
Tony Winning Moment · 38
Toots McGoots · 145
Top Charts · 136
Top That! · 201
Town Hall Meeting · 200
Try That On For Size · 201
TSA · 244
Two Chairs · 189
Two Lines · 68
Two Minute Expert · 201

## U

Ultra Extreme Five Things · 153
Ultra Naive Replay · 58
Uncle Gibberish · 79
Uncle Gibberish Switch · 79
Uncle Vanya · 79

## V

Vaudeville · 37
Voicemail · 229

## W

Wedding Planner · 155
Whale's Tale · 51
What Are You Doing? · 203
What If? · 98
What You Got? · 216
Whatcha Get? · 245
When I Grow Up · 246
Wikipedia (Challenge) · 202
Wikipedia (Conducted) · 186
Word At A Time Express · 190
Word From Our Sponsor · 99
World Without A Letter · 191
World's Worst · 247

## X

## Y

Yay Boo · 192
Yearbook · 139

## Z

Zombie Parade · 220

# WRITE YOUR OWN NOTES